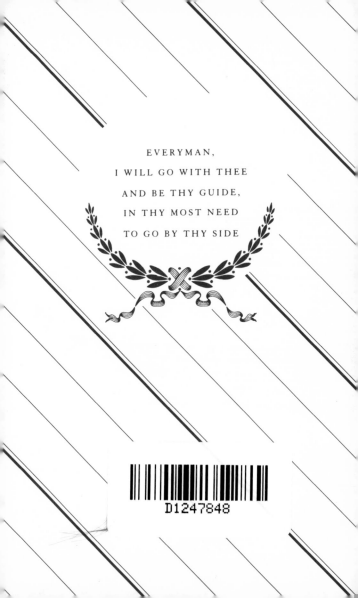

EVERYMAN,
I WILL GO WITH THEE
AND BE THY GUIDE,
IN THY MOST NEED
TO GO BY THY SIDE

EVERYMAN'S LIBRARY
POCKET POETS

MILTON

POEMS

EVERYMAN'S LIBRARY
POCKET POETS

This selection by Peter Washington first published in
Everyman's Library, 1996
© David Campbell Publishers Ltd., 1996

ISBN 1-85715-729-X

A CIP catalogue record for this book is available from the British Library

Published by David Campbell Publishers Ltd.,
79 Berwick Street, London W1V 3PF

Distributed by Random House (UK) Ltd.,
20 Vauxhall Bridge Road, London SW1V 2SA

Typography by Peter B. Willberg

Typeset by Acc Computing, Castle Cary, Somerset

Printed and bound in Germany by
Mohndruck Graphische Betriebe GmbH, Gütersloh

CONTENTS

JOHN
MILTON

········

POEMS

SONNETS

When I consider how my light is spent
   Ere half my days in this dark world and wide,
   And that one talent which is death to hide
   Lodged with me useless, though my soul more bent
To serve therewith my maker, and present
   My true account, lest he returning chide,
   'Doth God exact day-labour, light denied?'
   I fondly ask. But Patience, to prevent
That murmur, soon replies, 'God doth not need
   Either man's work or his own gifts; who best
   Bear his mild yoke, they serve him best: his state
Is kingly. Thousands at his bidding speed,
   And post o'er land and ocean without rest;
   They also serve who only stand and wait.'

O nightingale that on yon bloomy spray
 Warblest at eve, when all the woods are still,
 Thou with fresh hope the lover's heart dost fill,
 While the jolly hours lead on propitious May.
Thy liquid notes that close the eye of day,
 First heard before the shallow cuckoo's bill,
 Portend success in love. O, if Jove's will
 Have linked that amorous power to thy soft lay,
Now timely sing, ere the rude bird of hate
 Foretell my hopeless doom, in some grove nigh;
 As thou from year to year hast sung too late
For my relief, yet hadst no reason why.
 Whether the Muse or Love call thee his mate,
 Both them I serve, and of their train am I.

TO MR H. LAWES, ON HIS AIRS

Harry, whose tuneful and well-measured song
   First taught our English music how to span
   Words with just note and accent, not to scan
   With Midas' ears, committing short and long,
Thy worth and skill exempts thee from the throng,
   With praise enough for envy to look wan;
   To after age thou shalt be writ the man
     That with smooth air couldst humour best our
      tongue.
Thou honour'st verse, and verse must lend her wing
   To honour thee, the priest of Phoebus' choir,
   That tunest their happiest lines in hymn or story.
Dante shall give fame leave to set thee higher
   Than his Casella, whom he wooed to sing,
   Met in the milder shades of Purgatory.

How soon hath Time, the subtle thief of youth,
　　Stolen on his wing my three-and-twentieth year!
　　My hasting days fly on with full career,
　　But my late spring no bud or blossom sheweth.
Perhaps my semblance might deceive the truth,
　　That I to manhood am arrived so near;
　　And inward ripeness doth much less appear,
　　That some more timely-happy spirits endueth.
Yet, be it less or more, or soon or slow,
　　It shall be still in strictest measure even
　　To that same lot, however mean or high,
Toward which Time leads me, and the will of heaven,
　　All is, if I have grace to use it so,
　　As ever in my great task-master's eye.

Methought I saw my late espousèd saint
   Brought to me like Alcestis from the grave,
   Whom Jove's great son to her glad husband gave,
   Rescued from Death by force, though pale and faint.
Mine, as whom washed from spot of child-bed taint
   Purification in the old Law did save,
   And such as yet once more I trust to have
   Full sight of her in heaven without restraint,
Came vested all in white, pure as her mind.
   Her face was veiled; yet to my fancied sight
   Love, sweetness, goodness, in her person shined
So clear as in no face with more delight.
   But O as to embrace me she inclined,
   I waked, she fled, and day brought back my night.

ON THE RELIGIOUS MEMORY
OF MRS CATHERINE THOMASON,
MY CHRISTIAN FRIEND,
DECEASED DECEMBER 1646

When Faith and Love, which parted from thee never,
    Had ripened thy just soul to dwell with God,
    Meekly thou didst resign this earthly load
Of death, called life, which us from life doth sever.
Thy works, and alms, and all thy good endeavour,
    Stayed not behind, nor in the grave were trod;
    But, as Faith pointed with her golden rod,
Followed thee up to joy and bliss for ever.
Love led them on; and Faith, who knew them best
    Thy handmaids, clad them o'er with purple beams
    And azure wings, that up they flew so dressed,
And spake the truth of thee on glorious themes
    Before the judge; who thenceforth bid thee rest,
    And drink thy fill of pure immortal streams.

Lady, that in the prime of earliest youth
   Wisely hast shunned the broad way and the green,
   And with those few art eminently seen
   That labour up the hill of heavenly truth,
The better part with Mary and with Ruth,
   Chosen thou hast; and they that overween,
   And at thy growing virtues fret their spleen,
   No anger find in thee, but pity and ruth.
Thy care is fixed, and zealously attends
   To fill thy odorous lamp with deeds of light,
   And hope that reaps not shame. Therefore be sure
Thou, when the bridegroom with his feastful friends
   Passes to bliss at the mid-hour of night,
   Hast gained thy entrance, virgin wise and pure.

TO THE LADY MARGARET LEY

Daughter to that good Earl, once President
   Of England's Council and her Treasury,
   Who lived in both unstained with gold or fee,
   And left them both, more in himself content,
Till the sad breaking of that Parliament
   Broke him, as that dishonest victory
   At Chaeronea, fatal to liberty,
   Killed with report that old man eloquent,
Though later born than to have known the days
   Wherein your father flourished, yet by you,
   Madam, methinks I see him living yet;
So well your words his noble virtues praise
   That all both judge you to relate them true
   And to possess them, honoured Margaret.

Lawrence, of virtuous father virtuous son,
    Now that the fields are dank, and ways are mire,
    Where shall we sometimes meet, and by the fire
    Help waste a sullen day, what may be won
From the hard season gaining? Time will run
    On smoother, till Favonius reinspire
    The frozen earth, and clothe in fresh attire
    The lily and rose, that neither sowed nor spun.
What neat repast shall feast us, light and choice,
    Of Attic taste, with wine, whence we may rise,
    To hear the lute well touched, or artful voice
Warble immortal notes and Tuscan air?
    He who of those delights can judge, and spare
    To interpose them oft, is not unwise.

Cyriack, whose grandsire on the Royal Bench
　　Of British Themis, with no mean applause,
　　Pronounced, and in his volumes taught, our laws,
　　Which others at their bar so often wrench,
To-day deep thoughts resolve with me to drench
　　In mirth that after no repenting draws;
　　Let Euclid rest, and Archimedes pause,
　　And what the Swede intend, and what the French.
To measure life learn thou betimes, and know
　　Towards solid good what leads the nearest way;
　　For other things mild heaven a time ordains,
And disapproves that care, though wise in show,
　　That with superfluous burden loads the day,
　　And, when God sends a cheerful hour, refrains.

Cyriack, this three years' day these eyes, though clear,
    To outward view, of blemish or of spot,
    Bereft of light, their seeing have forgot;
    Nor to their idle orbs doth sight appear
Of sun, or moon, or star, throughout the year,
    Or man, or woman. Yet I argue not
    Against heaven's hand or will, nor bate a jot
    Of heart or hope, but still bear up and steer
Right onward. What supports me, dost thou ask?
    The conscience, friend, to have lost them overplied
    In liberty's defence, my noble task,
Of which all Europe talks from side to side.
    This thought might lead me through the world's
        vain mask
    Content, though blind, had I no better guide.

THE DETRACTION WHICH FOLLOWED
UPON MY WRITING CERTAIN TREATISES

A book was writ of late called *Tetrachordon*,
    And woven close, both matter, form, and style;
    The subject new: it walked the town a while,
    Numbering good intellects; now seldom pored on.
Cries the stall-reader, 'Bless us! what a word on
    A title-page is this!'; and some in file
    Stand spelling false, while one might walk to Mile-
    End Green. Why, is it harder, sirs, than Gordon,
Colkitto, or Macdonnel, or Galasp?
    Those rugged names to our like mouths grow sleek,
    That would have made Quintilian stare and gasp.
Thy age, like ours, O soul of Sir John Cheke,
    Hated not learning worse than toad or asp,
    When thou taught'st Cambridge and King Edward
        Greek.

ON THE SAME

I did but prompt the age to quit their clogs
   By the known rules of ancient liberty,
   When straight a barbarous noise environs me
   Of owls and cuckoos, asses, apes, and dogs;
As when those hinds that were transformed to frogs
   Railed at Latona's twin-born progeny,
   Which after held the sun and moon in fee.
   But this is got by casting pearl to hogs,
That bawl for freedom in their senseless mood,
   And still revolt when truth would set them free.
   Licence they mean when they cry liberty;
For who loves that must first be wise and good;
   But from that mark how far they rove we see,
   For all this waste of wealth and loss of blood.

ON THE NEW FORCERS OF CONSCIENCE
UNDER THE LONG PARLIAMENT

Because you have thrown off your prelate lord,
    And with stiff vows renounced his liturgy,
      To seize the widowed whore Plurality
    From them whose sin ye envied, not abhorred,
Dare ye for this adjure the civil sword
    To force our consciences that Christ set free,
      And ride us with a classic hierarchy,
    Taught ye by mere A. S. and Rutherford?
Men whose life, learning, faith, and pure intent,
    Would have been held in high esteem with Paul
    Must now be named and printed heretics
By shallow Edwards and Scotch what-d'ye-call!
    But we do hope to find out all your tricks,
    Your plots and packing, worse than those of Trent,
          That so the Parliament
May with their wholesome and preventive shears
Clip your phylacteries, though baulk your ears,
      And succour our just fears,
When they shall read this clearly in your charge:
New *Presbyter* is but old *Priest* writ large.

ON THE LATE MASSACRE IN PIEDMONT

Avenge, O Lord, thy slaughtered saints, whose bones
   Lie scattered on the Alpine mountains cold;
   Even them who kept thy truth so pure of old,
When all our fathers worshipped stocks and stones,
Forget not: in thy book record their groans
   Who were thy sheep, and in their ancient fold
   Slain by the bloody Piedmontese, that rolled
   Mother with infant down the rocks. Their moans
The vales redoubled to the hills, and they
   To heaven. Their martyred blood and ashes sow
   O'er all the Italian fields, where still doth sway
The triple Tyrant; that from these may grow
   A hundredfold, who, having learnt thy way,
   Early may fly the Babylonian woe.

TO THE LORD GENERAL CROMWELL, MAY 1652, ON THE PROPOSALS OF CERTAIN MINISTERS AT THE COMMITTEE FOR PROPAGATION OF THE GOSPEL

Cromwell, our chief of men, who through a cloud
    Not of war only, but detractions rude,
    Guided by faith and matchless fortitude,
    To peace and truth thy glorious way hast ploughed,
And on the neck of crownèd Fortune proud
    Hast reared God's trophies, and his work pursued,
    While Darwen stream, with blood of Scots imbrued,
    And Dunbar field resounds thy praises loud,
And Worcester's laureate wreath; yet much remains
    To conquer still; Peace hath her victories
    No less renowned than War: new foes arise,
Threatening to bind our souls with secular chains:
    Help us to save free conscience from the paw
    Of hireling wolves, whose gospel is their maw.

TO SIR HENRY VANE THE YOUNGER

Vane, young in years, but in sage counsel old,
   Than whom a better senator ne'er held
   The helm of Rome, when gowns, not arms, repelled
   The fierce Epirot, and the African bold;
Whether to settle peace, or to unfold
   The drift of hollow states hard to be spelled;
   Then to advise how war may best, upheld,
   Move by her two main nerves, iron and gold,
In all her equipage; besides, to know
   Both spiritual power and civil, what each means,
   What severs each, thou hast learned, which few have
     done.
The bounds of either sword to thee we owe;
   Therefore on thy firm hand Religion leans
   In peace, and reckons thee her eldest son.

ON THE LORD GENERAL FAIRFAX AT
THE SIEGE OF COLCHESTER

Fairfax, whose name in arms through Europe rings,
    Filling each mouth with envy or with praise,
    And all her jealous monarchs with amaze,
    And rumours loud that daunt remotest kings,
Thy firm unshaken virtue ever brings
    Victory home, though new rebellions raise
    Their hydra heads, and the false North displays
    Her broken league to imp their serpent wings.
O yet a nobler task awaits thy hand
    For what can war but endless war still breed
    Till truth and right from violence be freed,
And public faith cleared from the shameful brand
    Of public fraud. In vain doth Valour bleed,
    While Avarice and Rapine share the land.

OCCASIONAL POEMS

THE FIFTH ODE OF HORACE, LIB. I
Quis multâ gracilis te puer in rosâ.

Rendered almost word for word, without rhyme, according to the Latin measure, as near as the language will permit.

What slender youth, bedewed with liquid odours,
Courts thee on roses in some pleasant cave,
    Pyrrha? For whom bind'st thou
    In wreaths thy golden hair,
Plain in thy neatness? O how oft shall he
On faith and changèd gods complain, and seas
    Rough with black winds and storms
    Unwonted shall admire,
Who now enjoys thee credulous, all gold;
Who always vacant, always amiable,
    Hopes thee, of flattering gales
    Unmindful. Hapless they
To whom thou untried seem'st fair. Me, in my vowed
Picture, the sacred wall declares to have hung
    My dank and dropping weeds
    To the stern god of sea.

LYCIDAS

*In this monody the author bewails a learned friend,
unfortunately drowned in his passage from Chester on
the Irish Seas, 1637; and, by occasion, foretells the ruin
of our corrupted clergy, then in their height.*

Yet once more, O ye laurels, and once more
Ye myrtles brown, with ivy never sere,
I come to pluck your berries harsh and crude,
And with forced fingers rude
Shatter your leaves before the mellowing year.
Bitter constraint and sad occasion dear
Compels me to disturb your season due;
For Lycidas is dead, dead ere his prime,
Young Lycidas, and hath not left his peer.
Who would not sing for Lycidas? He knew
Himself to sing, and build the lofty rhyme.
He must not float upon his watery bier
Unwept, and welter to the parching wind,
Without the meed of some melodious tear.

    Begin, then, sisters of the sacred well
That from beneath the seat of Jove doth spring;
Begin, and somewhat loudly sweep the string.
Hence with denial vain and coy excuse;
So may some gentle muse
With lucky words favour my destined urn,
And as he passes turn,

And bid fair peace be to my sable shroud.

    For we were nursed upon the self-same hill,
Fed the same flock, by fountain, shade, and rill;
Together both, ere the high lawns appeared
Under the opening eyelids of the morn,
We drove a-field, and both together heard
What time the grey-fly winds her sultry horn,
Battening our flocks with the fresh dews of night,
Oft till the star that rose, at evening, bright,
Toward heaven's descent had sloped his westering wheel.
Meanwhile the rural ditties were not mute;
Tempered to the oaten flute,
Rough satyrs danced, and fauns with cloven heel
From the glad sound would not be absent long;
And old Damaetus loved to hear our song.

    But O the heavy change, now thou art gone,
Now thou art gone and never must return!
Thee, shepherd, thee the woods and desert caves,
With wild thyme and the gadding vine o'ergrown,
And all their echoes, mourn.
The willows, and the hazel copses green,
Shall now no more be seen
Fanning their joyous leaves to thy soft lays.
As killing as the canker to the rose,
Or taint-worm to the weanling herds that graze,
Or frost to flowers, that their gay wardrobe wear,
When first the white-thorn blows;

Such, Lycidas, thy loss to shepherd's ear.

    Where were ye, nymphs, when the remorseless deep
Closed o'er the head of your loved Lycidas?
For neither were ye playing on the steep
Where your old bards, the famous Druids, lie,
Nor on the shaggy top of Mona high,
Nor yet where Deva spreads her wizard stream.
Ay me! I fondly dream
'Had ye been there,' ... for what could that have done?
What could the muse herself that Orpheus bore,
The muse herself, for her enchanting son,
Whom universal nature did lament,
When, by the rout that made the hideous roar,
His gory visage down the stream was sent,
Down the swift Hebrus to the Lesbian shore?

    Alas! What boots it with uncessant care
To tend the homely slighted shepherd's trade,
And strictly meditate the thankless muse?
Were it not better done, as others use,
To sport with Amaryllis in the shade,
Or with the tangles of Neaera's hair?
Fame is the spur that the clear spirit doth raise
(That last infirmity of noble mind)
To scorn delights and live laborious days;
But the fair guerdon when we hope to find,
And think to burst out into sudden blaze,
Comes the blind Fury with the abhorrèd shears,

And slits the thin-spun life. 'But not the praise,'
Phoebus replied, and touched my trembling ears:
'Fame is no plant that grows on mortal soil,
Nor in the glistening foil
Set off to the world, nor in broad rumour lies,
But lives and spreads aloft by those pure eyes
And perfect witness of all-judging Jove;
As he pronounces lastly on each deed,
Of so much fame in heaven expect thy meed.'
   O fountain Arethuse, and thou honoured flood,
Smooth-sliding Mincius, crowned with vocal reeds,
That strain I heard was of a higher mood;
But now my oat proceeds,
And listens to the herald of the sea,
That came in Neptune's plea.
He asked the waves, and asked the felon winds,
What hard mishap hath doomed this gentle swain?
And questioned every gust of rugged wings
That blows from off each beakèd promontory:
They knew not of his story;
And sage Hippotades their answer brings,
That not a blast was from his dungeon strayed;
The air was calm, and on the level brine
Sleek Panope with all her sisters played.
It was that fatal and perfidious bark,
Built in the eclipse, and rigged with curses dark,
That sunk so low that sacred head of thine.

Next, Camus, reverend sire, went footing slow,
His mantle hairy, and his bonnet sedge,
Inwrought with figures dim, and on the edge
Like to that sanguine flower inscribed with woe.
'Ah! who hath reft,' quoth he, 'my dearest pledge?'
Last came, and last did go,
The pilot of the Galilean lake;
Two massy keys he bore of metals twain
(The golden opes, the iron shuts amain).
He shook his mitred locks, and stern bespake:
'How well could I have spared for thee, young swain,
Enow of such as, for their bellies' sake,
Creep, and intrude, and climb into the fold!
Of other care they little reckoning make
Than how to scramble at the shearers' feast,
And shove away the worthy bidden guest;
Blind mouths! That scarce themselves know how to hold
A sheep-hook, or have learned aught else the least
That to the faithful herdman's art belongs!
What recks it them? What need they? They are sped;
And, when they list, their lean and flashy songs
Grate on their scrannel pipes of wretched straw;
The hungry sheep look up, and are not fed,
But, swoll'n with wind and the rank mist they draw,
Rot inwardly, and foul contagion spread;
Besides what the grim wolf with privy paw
Daily devours apace, and nothing said.

But that two-handed engine at the door
Stands ready to smite once, and smite no more.'
    Return, Alpheus; the dread voice is past
That shrunk thy streams; return Sicilian muse,
And call the vales, and bid them hither cast
Their bells and flowerets of a thousand hues.
Ye valleys low, where the mild whispers use
Of shades, and wanton winds, and gushing brooks,
On whose fresh lap the swart star sparely looks,
Throw hither all your quaint enamelled eyes,
That on the green turf suck the honeyed showers,
And purple all the ground with vernal flowers.
Bring the rathe primrose that forsaken dies,
The tufted crow-toe, and pale jessamine,
The white pink, and the pansy freaked with jet,
The glowing violet,
The musk rose, and the well-attired woodbine,
With cowslips wan that hang the pensive head,
And every flower that sad embroidery wears;
Bid amaranthus all his beauty shed,
And daffadillies fill their cups with tears,
To strew the laureate hearse where Lycid lies.
For so, to interpose a little ease,
Let our frail thoughts dally with false surmise.
Ay me! Whilst thee the shores and sounding seas
Wash far away, where'er thy bones are hurled;
Whether beyond the stormy Hebrides,

Where thou perhaps under the whelming tide
Visit'st the bottom of the monstrous world;
Or whether thou, to our moist vows denied,
Sleep'st by the fable of Bellerus old,
Where the great vision of the guarded mount
Looks toward Namancos and Bayona's hold.
Look homeward, angel, now, and melt with ruth;
And, O ye dolphins, waft the hapless youth.

   Weep no more, woeful shepherds, weep no more,
For Lycidas, your sorrow, is not dead,
Sunk though he be beneath the watery floor.
So sinks the day-star in the ocean bed,
And yet anon repairs his drooping head,
And tricks his beams, and with new-spangled ore
Flames in the forehead of the morning sky:
So Lycidas sunk low, but mounted high,
Through the dear might of him that walked the waves,
Where, other groves and other streams along,
With nectar pure his oozy locks he laves,
And hears the unexpressive nuptial song,
In the blest kingdoms meek of joy and love.
There entertain him all the saints above,
In solemn troops, and sweet societies,
That sing, and singing in their glory move,
And wipe the tears for ever from his eyes.
Now, Lycidas, the shepherds weep no more;
Henceforth thou art the genius of the shore,

In thy large recompense, and shalt be good
To all that wander in that perilous flood.

   Thus sang the uncouth swain to the oaks and rills,
While the still morn went out with sandals grey;
He touched the tender stops of various quills;
With eager thought warbling his Doric lay:
And now the sun had stretched out all the hills,
And now was dropped into the western bay
At last he rose, and twitched his mantle blue:
To-morrow to fresh woods, and pastures new.

L'ALLEGRO

Hence, loathed Melancholy,
  Of Cerberus and blackest Midnight born
In Stygian cave forlorn
  'Mongst horrid shapes, and shrieks, and sights
    unholy;
Find out some uncouth cell,
  Where brooding Darkness spreads his jealous
    wings,
And the night-raven sings;
  There, under ebon shades and low-browed rocks,
As ragged as thy locks,
  In dark Cimmerian desert ever dwell.
But come, thou Goddess fair and free,
In heaven yclept Euphrosyne,
And by men, heart-easing Mirth;
Whom lovely Venus, at a birth,
With two sister Graces more,
To ivy-crownèd Bacchus bore;
Or whether (as some sager sing)
The frolic wind that breathes the spring,
Zephyr, with Aurora playing,
As he met her once a-Maying,
There, on beds of violets blue,
And fresh-blown roses washed in dew,
Filled her with thee, a daughter fair,

So buxom, blithe, and debonair.
Haste thee, Nymph, and bring with thee
Jest, and youthful Jollity,
Quips and cranks and wanton wiles,
Nods and becks and wreathèd smiles,
Such as hang on Hebe's cheek,
And love to live in dimple sleek;
Sport that wrinkled Care derides,
And Laughter holding both his sides.
Come, and trip it, as you go,
On the light fantastic toe;
And in thy right hand lead with thee
The mountain-nymph, sweet Liberty;
And, if I give thee honour due,
Mirth, admit me of thy crew,
To live with her, and live with thee,
In unreprovèd pleasures free;
To hear the lark begin his flight,
And, singing, startle the dull night,
From his watch-tower in the skies,
Till the dappled dawn doth rise;
Then to come, in spite of sorrow,
And at my window bid good-morrow,
Through the sweet-briar or the vine,
Or the twisted eglantine;
While the cock, with lively din,
Scatters the rear of darkness thin;

And to the stack, or the barn-door,
Stoutly struts his dames before,
Oft listening how the hounds and horn
Cheerly rouse the slumbering morn,
From the side of some hoar hill,
Through the high wood echoing shrill.
Sometime walking, not unseen,
By hedgerow elms, on hillocks green,
Right against the eastern gate
Where the great sun begins his state,
Robed in flames and amber light,
The clouds in thousand liveries dight;
While the ploughman, near at hand,
Whistles o'er the furrowed land,
And the milkmaid singeth blithe,
And the mower whets his scythe,
And every shepherd tells his tale
Under the hawthorn in the dale.
Straight mine eye hath caught new pleasures,
Whilst the landscape round it measures:
Russet lawns, and fallows grey,
Where the nibbling flocks do stray;
Mountains on whose barren breast
The labouring clouds do often rest;
Meadows trim, with daisies pied,
Shallow brooks, and rivers wide.
Towers and battlements it sees

Bosomed high in tufted trees,
Where perhaps some beauty lies,
The cynosure of neighbouring eyes.
Hard by a cottage chimney smokes
From betwixt two aged oaks.
Where Corydon and Thyrsis met
Are at their savoury dinner set
Of herbs and other country messes,
Which the neat-handed Phyllis dresses;
And then in haste her bower she leaves,
With Thestylis to bind the sheaves;
Or, if the earlier season lead,
To the tanned haycock in the mead.
Sometimes, with secure delight,
The upland hamlets will invite,
When the merry bells ring round,
And the jocund rebecks sound
To many a youth and many a maid
Dancing in the chequered shade,
And young and old come forth to play
On a sunshine holiday,
Till the livelong daylight fail,
Then to a spicy nut-brown ale,
With stories told of many a feat,
How Fairy Mab the junkets eat;
She was pinched and pulled, she said,
And by the friar's lantern led,

Tells how the drudging goblin sweat
To earn his cream-bowl duly set,
When in one night, ere glimpse of morn,
His shadowy flail hath threshed the corn
That ten day-labourers could not end;
Then lies him down, the lubber fiend,
And, stretched out all the chimney's length
Basks at the fire his hairy strength,
And crop-full out of doors he flings,
Ere the first cock his matin rings.
Thus done the tales, to bed they creep,
By whispering winds soon lulled asleep.
Towered cities please us then,
And the busy hum of men,
Where throngs of knights and barons hold,
In weeds of peace, high triumphs hold,
With store of ladies, whose bright eyes
Rain influence, and judge the prize
Of wit or arms, while both contend
To win her grace whom all commend.
There let Hymen oft appear
In saffron robe, with taper clear,
And pomp, and feast, and revelry.
With mask and antique pageantry;
Such sights as youthful poets dream
On summer eves by haunted stream.
Then to the well-trod stage anon,

If Jonson's learned sock be on,
Or sweetest Shakespeare, Fancy's child,
Warble his native wood-notes wild.
And ever, against eating cares,
Lap me in soft Lydian airs,
Married to immortal verse,
Such as the meeting soul may pierce,
In notes with many a winding bout
Of linkèd sweetness long drawn out
With wanton heed and giddy cunning,
The melting voice through mazes running,
Untwisting all the chains that tie
The hidden soul of harmony.
That Orpheus' self may heave his head
From golden slumber on a bed
Of heaped Elysian flowers, and hear
Such strains as would have won the ear
Of Pluto to have quite set free
His half-regained Eurydice.
These delights if thou canst give,
Mirth, with thee I mean to live.

IL PENSEROSO

Hence, vain deluding Joys,
    The brood of Folly without father bred,
How little you bestead,
    Or fill the fixèd mind with all your toys;
Dwell in some idle brain,
    And fancies fond with gaudy shapes possess,
As thick and numberless
    As the gay motes that people the sunbeams,
Or likest hovering dreams,
    The fickle pensioners of Morpheus' train.
But, hail thou goddess, sage and holy,
Hail, divinest Melancholy,
Whose saintly visage is too bright
To hit the sense of human sight,
And therefore to our weaker view
O'erlaid with black, staid wisdom's hue.
Black, but such as in esteem
Prince Memnon's sister might beseem,
Or that starred Ethiop queen that strove
To set her beauty's praise above
The sea-nymphs, and their powers offended;
Yet thou art higher far descended,
Thee bright-haired Vesta long of yore
To solitary Saturn bore;
His daughter she (in Saturn's reign

Such mixture was not held a stain),
Oft in glimmering bowers and glades
He met her, and in secret shades
Of woody Ida's inmost grove,
Whilst yet there was no fear of Jove.
Come, pensive nun, devout and pure,
Sober, steadfast and demure,
All in a robe of darkest grain,
Flowing with majestic train,
And sable stole of cypress lawn
Over thy decent shoulders drawn.
Come, but keep thy wonted state,
With even step, and musing gait,
And looks commercing with the skies,
Thy rapt soul sitting in thine eyes:
There, held in holy passion still,
Forget thyself to marble, till
With a sad leaden downward cast
Thou fix them on the earth as fast.
And join with thee calm Peace and Quiet,
Spare Fast, that oft with gods doth diet,
And hears the Muses in a ring
Aye round about Jove's altar sing.
And add to these retired Leisure,
That in trim gardens takes his pleasure;
But, first and chiefest, with thee bring
Him that yon soars on golden wing,

Guiding the fiery-wheelèd throne,
The cherub Contemplation;
And the mute Silence hist along,
'Less Philomel will deign a song,
In her sweetest saddest plight,
Smoothing the rugged brow of Night,
While Cynthia checks her dragon yoke
Gently o'er the accustomed oak.
Sweet bird, that shunn'st the noise of folly,
Most musical, most melancholy!
Thee, chauntress, oft the woods among
I woo, to hear thy even-song;
And, missing thee, I walk unseen
On the dry smooth-shaven green
To behold the wandering moon,
Riding near her highest noon,
Like one that had been led astray
Through the heaven's wide pathless way,
And oft, as if her head she bowed,
Stooping through a fleecy cloud.
Oft, on a plat of rising ground,
I hear the far-off curfew sound,
Over some wide-watered shore,
Swinging slow with sullen roar;
Or, if the air will not permit,
Some still removèd place will fit,
Where glowing embers through the room

Teach light to counterfeit a gloom,
Far from all resort of mirth,
Save the cricket on the hearth,
Or the bellman's drowsy charm
To bless the doors from nightly harm;
Or let my lamp, at midnight hour,
Be seen in some high lonely tower,
Where I may oft outwatch the Bear,
With thrice great Hermes, or unsphere
The spirit of Plato, to unfold
What worlds or what past regions hold
The immortal mind that hath forsook
Her mansion in this fleshly nook;
And of those demons that are found
In fire, air, flood, or underground,
Whose power hath a true consent
With planet or with element.
Sometimes let gorgeous Tragedy
In sceptered pall come sweeping by,
Presenting Thebes, or Pelops' line,
Or the tale of Troy divine,
Or what (though rare) of later age
Ennobled hath the buskined stage.
But, O sad Virgin, that thy power
Might raise Musaeus from his bower;
Or bid the soul of Orpheus sing
Such notes as, warbled to the string,

Drew iron tears down Pluto's cheek,
And made hell grant what love did seek;
Or call up him that left half-told
The story of Cambuscan bold,
Of Camball, and of Algarsife,
And who had Canace to wife,
That owned the virtuous ring and glass,
And of the wondrous horse of brass
On which the Tartar king did ride;
And if aught else great bards beside
In sage and solemn tunes have sung,
Of tourneys, and of trophies hung,
Of forests, and enchantments drear,
Where more is meant than meets the ear;
Thus, Night, oft see me in thy pale career,
Till civil-suited Morn appear,
Not tricked and frounced, as she was wont
With the Attic boy to hunt,
But kerchiefed in a comely cloud,
While rocking winds are piping loud,
Or ushered with a shower still,
When the gust hath blown his fill,
Ending on the rustling leaves,
With minute-drops from off the eaves.
And, when the sun begins to fling
His flaring beams, me, goddess, bring
To archèd walks of twilight groves,

And shadows brown, that Sylvan loves,
Of pine, or monumental oak,
Where the rude axe with heavèd stroke
Was never heard the nymphs to daunt,
Or fright them from their hallowed haunt.
There, in close covert, by some brook,
Where no profaner eye may look,
Hide me from day's garish eye,
While the bee with honeyed thigh,
That at her flowery work doth sing,
And the waters murmuring,
With such consort as they keep,
Entice the dewy-feathered Sleep;
And let some strange mysterious dream
Wave at his wings, in airy stream
Of lively portraiture displayed,
Softly on my eyelids laid;
And, as I wake, sweet music breathe
Above, about, or underneath,
Sent by some spirit to mortals good,
Or the unseen genius of the wood.
But let my due feet never fail
To walk the studious cloister's pale,
And love the high embowèd roof,
With antique pillars' massy-proof,
And storied windows richly dight,
Casting a dim religious light.

There let the pealing organ blow,
To the full-voiced choir below,
In service high and anthems clear,
As may with sweetness, through mine ear,
Dissolve me into ecstasies,
And bring all heaven before mine eyes.
And may at last my weary age
Find out the peaceful hermitage,
The hairy gown and mossy cell,
Where I may sit and rightly spell
Of every star that heaven doth show,
And every herb that sips the dew,
Till old experience do attain
To something like prophetic strain.
These pleasures, Melancholy, give;
And I with thee will choose to live.

AT A SOLEMN MUSIC

Blest pair of sirens, pledges of heaven's joy,
Sphere-born harmonious sisters, Voice and Verse,
Wed your divine sounds, and mixed power employ,
Dead things with inbreathed sense able to pierce,
And to our high-raised fantasy present
That undisturbèd song of pure concent,
Aye sung before the sapphire-coloured throne
To him that sits thereon,
With saintly shout and solemn jubilee;
Where the bright seraphim in burning row
Their loud uplifted angel-trumpets blow,
And the cherubic host in thousand choirs
Touch their immortal harps of golden wires,
With those just spirits that wear victorious palms,
Hymns devout and holy psalms
Singing everlastingly;

That we on earth, with undiscording voice,
May rightly answer that melodious noise;
As once we did, till disproportioned sin
Jarred against nature's chime, and with harsh din
Broke the fair music that all creatures made
To their great Lord, whose love their motion swayed
In perfect diapason, whilst they stood
In first obedience, and their state of good.
O may we soon again renew that song,
And keep in tune with heaven, till God ere long
To his celestial consort us unite,
To live with him, and sing in endless morn of light.

ON SHAKESPEARE. 1630

What needs my Shakespeare for his honoured bones
The labour of an age in pilèd stones?
Or that his hallowed relics should be hid
Under a star-ypointing pyramid?
Dear son of memory, great heir of fame,
What need'st thou such weak witness of thy name?
Thou in our wonder and astonishment
Has built thyself a livelong monument.
For whilst, to the shame of slow-endeavouring art,
Thy easy numbers flow, and that each heart
Hath from the leaves of thy unvalued book
Those Delphic lines with deep impression took,
Then thou, our fancy of itself bereaving,
Dost make us marble with too much conceiving,
And so sepúlchred in such pomp dost lie
That kings for such a tomb would wish to die.

ON THE UNIVERSITY CARRIER

Who sickened in the time of his Vacancy, being forbid to go to London by reason of the Plague

Here lies old Hobson; Death hath broke his girt,
And here, alas, hath laid him in the dirt;
Or else, the way being foul, twenty to one
He's here stuck in a slough, and overthrown.
'Twas such a shifter that, if truth were known,
Death was half glad when he had got him down;
For he had any time this ten years full
Dodged with him betwixt Cambridge and the Bull.
And surely Death could never have prevailed,
Had not his weekly course of carriage failed;
But lately, finding him so long at home,
And thinking now his journey's end was come,
And that he had ta'en up his latest inn,
In the kind office of a chamberlain
Showed him his room where he must lodge that night,
Pulled off his boots, and took away the light.
If any ask for him, it shall be said,
'Hobson has supped, and's newly gone to bed.'

From COMUS

THE PERSONS

The ATTENDANT SPIRIT,   THE LADY.
    afterwards in the habit   FIRST BROTHER.
    of THYRSIS.   SECOND BROTHER.
COMUS, with his Crew.   SABRINA, the Nymph.

The Chief Persons which presented were:

> The Lord Brackley;
> Mr Thomas Egerton, his Brother;
> The Lady Alice Egerton.

The first Scene discovers a wild wood.

The ATTENDANT SPIRIT *descends or enters.*

Before the starry threshold of Jove's court
My mansion is, where those immortal shapes
Of bright aerial spirits live ensphered
In regions mild of calm and serene air,
Above the smoke and stir of this dim spot
Which men call earth, and, with low-thoughted care,
Confined and pestered in this pinfold here,
Strive to keep up a frail and feverish being
Unmindful of the crown that virtue gives,
After this mortal change, to her true servants
Amongst the enthroned gods on sainted seats.
Yet some there be that by due steps aspire
To lay their just hands on that golden key
That opes the palace of eternity:
To such my errand is; and but for such,
I would not soil these pure ambrosial weeds
With the rank vapours of this sin-worn mould.
    But to my task. Neptune, besides the sway
Of every salt flood and each ebbing stream,
Took in by lot, 'twixt high and nether Jove,
Imperial rule of all the sea-girt isles
That, like to rich and various gems, inlay
The unadornèd bosom of the deep;
Which he, to grace his tributary gods,
By course commits to several government,
And gives them leave to wear their sapphire crowns
And wield their little tridents; but this isle,

The greatest and the best of all the main,
He quarters to his blue-haired deities;
And all this tract that fronts the falling sun
A noble peer of mickle trust and power
Has in his charge, with tempered awe to guide
An old and haughty nation, proud in arms:
Where his fair offspring, nursed in princely lore,
Are coming to attend their father's state,
And new-entrusted sceptre; but their way
Lies through the perplexed paths of this drear wood,
The nodding horror of whose shady brows
Threats the forlorn and wandering passenger;
And here their tender age might suffer peril,
But that, by quick command from sovereign Jove,
I was despatched for their defence and guard:
And listen why; for I will tell you now
What never yet was heard in tale or song,
From old or modern bard, in hall or bower.

    Bacchus, that first from out the purple grape
Crushed the sweet poison of misusèd wine,
After the Tuscan mariners transformed,
Coasting the Tyrrhene shore, as the winds listed,
On Circe's island fell. (Who knows not Circe,
The daughter of the Sun, whose charmèd cup
Whoever tasted lost his upright shape,
And downward fell into a grovelling swine?)
This Nymph, that gazed upon his clustering locks,

With ivy berries wreathed, and his blithe youth,
Had by him, ere he parted thence, a son
Much like his father, but his mother more,
Whom therefore she brought up, and Comus named:
Who, ripe and frolic of his full-grown age,
Roving the Celtic and Iberian fields,
At last betakes him to this ominous wood,
And, in thick shelter of black shades embowered,
Excels his mother at her mighty art,
Offering to every weary traveller
His orient liquor in a crystal glass,
To quench the drought of Phoebus; which as they taste
(For most do taste through fond intemperate thirst),
Soon as the potion works, their human countenance,
The express resemblance of the gods, is changed
Into some brutish form of wolf or bear,
Or ounce or tiger, hog, or bearded goat,
All other parts remaining as they were,
And they, so perfect in their misery,
Not once perceive their foul disfigurement,
But boast themselves more comely than before,
And all their friends and native home forget,
To roll with pleasure in a sensual sty.
Therefore, when any favoured of high Jove
Chances to pass through this adventurous glade,
Swift as the sparkle of a glancing star
I shoot from heaven, to give him safe convoy,

As now I do; but first I must put off
These my sky-robes, spun out of Iris' woof,
And take the weeds and likeness of a swain
That to the service of this house belongs,
Who, with his soft pipe and smooth-dittied song,
Well knows to still the wild winds when they roar,
And hush the waving woods; nor of less faith,
And in this office of his mountain watch
Likeliest, and nearest to the present aid
Of this occasion. But I hear the tread
Of hateful steps; I must be viewless now.

(Lines 1–92)

SONG

Sweet Echo, sweetest nymph, that liv'st unseen
   Within thy airy shell
  By slow Meander's margent green,
And in the violet-embroidered vale
   Where the love-lorn nightingale
Nightly to thee her sad song mourneth well.
Canst thou not tell me of a gentle pair
   That likest thy Narcissus are?
    O, if thou have
   Hid them in some flowery cave,
    Tell me but where,
  Sweet queen of parley, daughter of the sphere!
  So may'st thou be translated to the skies,
And give resounding grace to all heaven's harmonies.

        (Lines 230–243)

Eld.Bro. My sister is not so defenceless left
As you imagine; she has a hidden strength,
Which you remember not.
    Sec. Bro.   What hidden strength,
Unless the strength of heaven, if you mean that?
    Eld. Bro. I mean that too, but yet a hidden strength,
Which, if heaven gave it, may be termed her own.
'Tis chastity, my brother, chastity:
She that has that is clad in complete steel,
And, like a quivered nymph with arrows keen,
May trace huge forests, and unharboured heaths,
Infamous hills, and sandy perilous wilds;
Where, through the sacred rays of chastity,
No savage fierce, bandit, or mountaineer,
Will dare to soil her virgin purity.
Yea, there where very desolation dwells,
By grots and caverns shagged with horrid shades,
She may pass on with unblenched majesty,
Be it not done in pride, or in presumption.
Some say no evil thing that walks by night,
In fog or fire, by lake or moorish fen,
Blue meagre hag, or stubborn unlaid ghost,
That breaks his magic chains at curfew time,
No goblin or swart fairy of the mine,
Hath hurtful power o'er true virginity.
Do ye believe me yet, or shall I call
Antiquity from the old schools of Greece

To testify the arms of chastity?
Hence had the huntress Dian her dread bow,
Fair silver-shafted queen for ever chaste,
Wherewith she tamed the brinded lioness
And spotted mountain-pard, but set at nought
The frivolous bow of Cupid; gods and men
Feared her stern frown, and she was queen o' the woods.
What was the snaky-headed Gorgon shield
That wise Minerva wore, unconquered virgin,
Wherewith she freezed her foes to congealed stone,
But rigid looks of chaste austerity,
And noble grace that dashed brute violence
With sudden adoration and blank awe?
So dear to heaven is saintly chastity
That, when a soul is found sincerely so,
A thousand liveried angels lackey her,
Driving far off each thing of sin and guilt,
And in clear dream and solemn vision
Tell her of things that no gross ear can hear;
Till oft converse with heavenly habitants
Begin to cast a beam on the outward shape,
The unpolluted temple of the mind,
And turns it by degrees to the soul's essence,
Till all be made immortal. But when lust,
By unchaste looks, loose gestures, and foul talk,
But most by lewd and lavish act of sin,
Lets in defilement to the inward parts,

The soul grows clotted by contagion,
Embodies, and imbrutes, till she quite lose
The divine property of her first being.
Such are those thick and gloomy shadows damp
Oft seen in charnel-vaults and sepulchres,
Lingering and sitting by a new-made grave,
As loath to leave the body that it loved,
And linked itself by carnal sensualty
To a degenerate and degraded state.
   Sec. Bro. How charming is divine philosophy!
Not harsh and crabbed, as dull fools suppose,
But musical as is Apollo's lute,
And a perpetual feast of nectared sweets,
Where no crude surfeit reigns.

(Lines 414–479)

*

Within the navel of this hideous wood,
Immured in cypress shades, a sorcerer dwells,
Of Bacchus and of Circe born, great Comus,
Deep skilled in all his mother's witcheries,
And here to every thirsty wanderer
By sly enticement gives his baneful cup,
With many murmurs mixed, whose pleasing poison
The visage quite transforms of him that drinks,
And the inglorious likeness of a beast

Fixes instead, unmoulding reason's mintage
Charactered in the face; this have I learnt
Tending my flocks hard by i' the hilly crofts
That brow this bottom glade, whence night by night
He and his monstrous rout are heard to howl
Like stabled wolves, or tigers at their prey,
Doing abhorred rites to Hecate
In their obscurèd haunts of inmost bowers;
Yet have they many baits and guileful spells
To inveigle and invite the unwary sense
Of them that pass unweeting by the way.
This evening late, by then the chewing flocks
Had ta'en their supper on the savoury herb
Of knot-grass dew-besprent, and were in fold,
I sat me down to watch upon a bank
With ivy canopied, and interwove
With flaunting honeysuckle, and began,
Wrapped in a pleasing fit of melancholy,
To meditate my rural minstrelsy,
Till fancy had her fill; but ere a close
The wonted roar was up amidst the woods,
And filled the air with barbarous dissonance
At which I ceased, and listened them a while,
Till an unusual stop of sudden silence
Gave respite to the drowsy-flighted steeds
That draw the litter of close-curtained sleep.
At last a soft and solemn-breathing sound

Rose like a steam of rich distilled perfumes,
And stole upon the air, that even Silence
Was took ere she was ware, and wished she might
Deny her nature, and be never more,
Still to be so displaced. I was all ear,
And took in strains that might create a soul
Under the ribs of Death. But O ere long
Too well I did perceive it was the voice
Of my most honoured Lady, your dear sister.
Amazed I stood, harrowed with grief and fear;
And 'O poor hapless nightingale,' thought I,
'How sweet thou sing'st, how near the deadly snare!'
Then down the lawns I ran with headlong haste,
Through paths and turnings often trod by day,
Till, guided by mine ear, I found the place
Where that damned wizard, hid in sly disguise
(For so by certain signs I knew), had met
Already, ere my best speed could prevent,
The aidless innocent Lady, his wished prey,
Who gently asked if he had seen such two,
Supposing him some neighbour villager;
Longer I durst not stay, but soon I guessed
Ye were the two she meant; with that I sprung
Into swift flight, till I had found you here;
But further know I not.

(Lines 520–580)

Lady. I hate when vice can bolt her arguments
And virtue has no tongue to check her pride.
Impostor! Do not charge most innocent Nature,
As if she would her children should be riotous
With her abundance. She, good cateress,
Means her provision only to the good,
That live according to her sober laws,
And holy dictate of spare Temperance.
If every just man that now pines with want
Had but a moderate and beseeming share
Of that which lewdly-pampered Luxury
Now heaps upon some few with vast excess,
Nature's full blessings would be well-dispensed
In unsuperfluous even proportion,
And she no whit encumbered with her store;
And then the giver would be better thanked
His praise due paid: for swinish gluttony
Ne'er looks to heaven amidst his gorgeous feast,
But with besotted base ingratitude
Crams, and blasphemes his feeder. Shall I go on?
Or have I said enough? To him that dares
Arm his profane tongue with contemptuous words
Against the sun-clad power of chastity
Fain would I something say – yet to what end?
Thou hast nor ear, nor soul, to apprehend
The sublime notion and high mystery
That must be uttered to unfold the sage

And serious doctrine of Virginity;
And thou art worthy that thou shouldst not know
More happiness than this thy present lot.
Enjoy your dear wit, and gay rhetoric,
That hath so well been taught her dazzling fence;
Thou art not fit to hear thyself convinced.
Yet, should I try, the uncontrollèd worth
Of this pure cause would kindle my rapt spirits
To such a flame of sacred vehemence
That dumb things would be moved to sympathise,
And the brute Earth would lend her nerves, and shake,
Till all thy magic structures, reared so high,
Were shattered into heaps o'er thy false head.

(Lines 760–799)

*

Spirit. There is a gentle Nymph not far from hence,
That with moist curb sways the smooth Severn stream:
Sabrina is her name, a virgin pure;
Whilom she was the daughter of Locrine,
That had the sceptre from his father Brute.
She, guileless damsel, flying the mad pursuit
Of her enragèd stepdame, Guendolen,
Commended her fair innocence to the flood
That stayed her flight with his cross-flowing course;
The water-nymphs, that in the bottom played,

Held up their pearlèd wrists, and took her in,
Bearing her straight to aged Nereus' hall,
Who, piteous of her woes, reared her lank head,
And gave her to his daughters to imbathe
In nectared lavers strewed with asphodel,
And through the porch and inlet of each sense
Dropped in ambrosial oils, till she revived,
And underwent a quick immortal change,
Made goddess of the river; still she retains
Her maiden gentleness, and oft at eve
Visits the herds along the twilight meadows,
Helping all urchin blasts, and ill-luck signs
That the shrewd meddling elf delights to make,
Which she with precious vialed liquors heals.
For which the shepherds at their festivals
Carol her goodness loud in rustic lays,
And throw sweet garland wreaths into her stream
Of pansies, pinks, and gaudy daffodils.
And, as the old swain said, she can unlock
The clasping charm, and thaw the numbing spell,
If she be right invoked in warbled song;
For maidenhood she loves, and will be swift
To aid a virgin, such as was herself,
In hard-besetting need; this will I try,
And add the power of some adjuring verse.

(Lines 824–858)

From
SAMSON AGONISTES

THE PERSONS

SAMSON.

MANOA, the father of
Samson.

DALILA, his wife.

HARAPHA of Gath.

Public Officer.

Messenger.

Chorus of Danites.

The Scene, before the Prison in Gaza.

Sams. A little onward lend thy guiding hand
To these dark steps, a little further on;
For yonder bank hath choice of sun or shade;
There I am wont to sit, when any chance
Relieves me from my task of servile toil,
Daily in the common prison else enjoined me,
Where I, a prisoner chained, scarce freely draw
The air, imprisoned also, close and damp,
Unwholesome draught; but here I feel amends –
The breath of heaven fresh blowing, pure and sweet,
With day-spring born; here leave me to respire.
This day a solemn feast the people hold
To Dagon, their sea-idol, and forbid
Laborious works; unwillingly this rest
Their superstition yields me; hence, with leave
Retiring from the popular noise, I seek
This unfrequented place, to find some ease –
Ease to the body some, none to the mind
From restless thoughts, that like a deadly swarm
Of hornets armed, no sooner found alone
But rush upon me thronging, and present
Times past, what once I was, and what am now.
Oh, wherefore was my birth from heaven foretold
Twice by an angel, who at last, in sight
Of both my parents, all in flames ascended
From off the altar where an offering burned,
As in a fiery column charioting

His godlike presence, and from some great act
Or benefit revealed to Abraham's race?
Why was my breeding ordered and prescribed
As of a person separate to God,
Designed for great exploits, if I must die
Betrayed, captived, and both my eyes put out,
Made of my enemies the scorn and gaze,
To grind in brazen fetters under task
With this heaven-gifted strength? O glorious strength,
Put to the labour of a beast, debased
Lower than bond-slave! Promise was that I
Should Israel from Philistian yoke deliver;
Ask for this great deliverer now, and find him
Eyeless in Gaza, at the mill with slaves,
Himself in bonds under Philistian yoke;
Yet stay; let me not rashly call in doubt
Divine prediction; what if all foretold
Had been fulfilled but through mine own default?
Whom have I to complain of but myself?
Who this high gift of strength committed to me,
In what part lodged, how easily bereft me,
Under the seal of silence could not keep,
But weakly to a woman must reveal it,
O'ercome with importunity and tears?
O impotence of mind in body strong!
But what is strength without a double share
Of wisdom? Vast, unwieldy, burdensome,

Proudly secure, yet liable to fall
By weakest subtleties; not made to rule,
But to subserve where wisdom bears command.
God, when he gave me strength, to show withal,
How slight the gift was, hung it in my hair.
But peace, I must not quarrel with the will
Of highest dispensation, which herein
Haply had ends above my reach to know;
Suffices that to me strength is my bane,
And proves the source of all my miseries –
So many, and so huge, that each apart
Would ask a life to wail; but, chief of all,
O loss of sight, of thee I most complain!
Blind among enemies, O worse than chains,
Dungeon, or beggary, or decrepit age!
Light, the prime work of God, to me is extinct,
And all her various objects of delight
Annulled, which might in part my grief have eased;
Inferior to the vilest now become
Of man or worm, the vilest here excel me:
They creep, yet see; I, dark in light, exposed
To daily fraud, contempt, abuse, and wrong,
Within doors, or without, still as a fool,
In power of others, never in my own –
Scarce half I seem to live, dead more than half.
O dark, dark, dark, amid the blaze of noon,
Irrecoverably dark, total eclipse

Without all hope of day!
O first-created beam, and thou great word,
'Let there be light, and light was over all,'
Why am I thus bereaved thy prime decree?
The sun to me is dark
And silent as the moon,
When she deserts the night,
Hid in her vacant interlunar cave.
Since light so necessary is to life,
And almost life itself, if it be true
That light is in the soul,
She all in every part, why was the sight
To such a tender ball as the eye confined,
So obvious and so easy to be quenched,
And not, as feeling, through all parts diffused,
That she might look at will through every pore?
Then had I not been thus exiled from light,
As in the land of darkness, yet in light,
To live a life half dead, a living death,
And buried; but O yet more miserable!
Myself my sepulchre, a moving grave;
Buried, yet not exempt,
By privilege of death and burial,
From worst of other evils, pains, and wrongs;
But made hereby obnoxious more
To all the miseries of life,
Life in captivity

Among inhuman foes.
But who are these? For with joint pace I hear
The tread of many feet steering this way;
Perhaps my enemies, who come to stare
At my affliction, and perhaps to insult –
Their daily practice to afflict me more.
   Chor. This, this is he; softly a while;
Let us not break in upon him;
O change beyond report, thought, or belief!
See how he lies at random, carelessly diffused,
With languished head unpropped,
As one past hope, abandoned,
And by himself given over,
In slavish habit, ill-fitted weeds
O'er-worn and soiled;
Or do my eyes misrepresent? Can this be he,
That heroic, that renowned,
Irresistible Samson? Whom, unarmed,
No strength of man, or fiercest wild beast,
    could withstand;
Who tore the lion as the lion tears the kid;
Ran on embattled armies clad in iron,
And, weaponless himself,
Made arms ridiculous, useless the forgery
Of brazen shield and spear, the hammered cuirass,
Chalybean-tempered steel, and frock of mail
Adamantean proof;

But safest he who stood aloof,
When insupportably his foot advanced,
In scorn of their proud arms and warlike tools,
Spurned them to death by troops. The bold Ascalonite
Fled from his lion ramp; old warriors turned
Their plated backs under his heel,
Or grovelling soiled their crested helmets in the dust.
Then with what trivial weapon came to hand,
The jaw of a dead ass, his sword of bone,
A thousand foreskins fell, the flower of Palestine,
In Ramath-lechi, famous to this day:
Then by main force pulled up, and on his shoulders bore,
The gates of Azza, post and massy bar,
Up to the hill by Hebron, seat of giants old –
No journey of a sabbath-day, and loaded so –
Like whom the Gentiles feign to bear up heaven.
Which shall I first bewail –
Thy bondage or lost sight,
Prison within prison
Inseparably dark?
Thou art become (O worst imprisonment!)
The dungeon of thyself; thy soul,
(Which men enjoying sight oft without cause complain)
Imprisoned now indeed,
In real darkness of the body dwells,
Shut up from outward light
To incorporate with gloomy night;

For inward light, alas,
Puts forth no visual beam.
O mirror of our fickle state,
Since man on earth, unparalleled!
The rarer thy example stands,
By how much from the top of wondrous glory,
Strongest of mortal men,
To lowest pitch of abject fortune thou art fallen.
For him I reckon not in high estate
Whom long descent of birth,
Or the sphere of fortune, raises;
But thee, whose strength, while virtue was her mate,
Might have subdued the earth,
Universally crowned with highest praises.

(Lines 1–175)

Chor. Just are the ways of God,
And justifiable to men,
Unless there be who think not God at all;
If any be, they walk obscure:
For of such doctrine never was there school,
But the heart of the fool,
And no man therein doctor but himself.
　　Yet more there be who doubt his ways not just,
As to his own edicts found contradicting;
Then give the reins to wandering thought,
Regardless of his glory's diminution,
Till, by their own perplexities involved,
They ravel more, still less resolved,
But never find self-satisfying solution.
　　As if they would confine the interminable,
And tie him to his own prescript,
Who made our laws to bind us, not himself,
And hath full right to exempt
Whomso it pleases him by choice
From national obstriction, without taint
Of sin, or legal debt;
For with his own laws he can best dispense.

(Lines 293–314)

Chor. God of our fathers, what is man,
That thou towards him with hand so various –
Or might I say contrarious? –
Temper'st thy providence through his short course:
Not evenly, as thou rul'st
The angelic orders, and inferior creatures mute,
Irrational and brute?
Nor do I name of men the common rout,
That, wandering loose about,
Grow up and perish as the summer fly,
Heads without name, no more remembered;
But such as thou hast solemnly elected,
With gifts and graces eminently adorned,
To some great work, thy glory,
And people's safety, which in part they effect;
Yet toward these, thus dignified, thou oft,
Amidst their height of noon,
Changest thy countenance and thy hand,
    with no regard
Of highest favours past
From thee on them, or them to thee of service.
  Nor only dost degrade them, or remit
To life obscured, which were a fair dismission,
But throw'st them lower than thou didst exalt
    them high –
Unseemly falls in human eye,
Too grievous for the trespass or omission;

Oft leav'st them to the hostile sword
Of heathen and profane, their carcasses
To dogs and fowls a prey, or else captived,
Or to the unjust tribunals, under change of times,
And condemnation of the ingrateful multitude.
If these they scape, perhaps in poverty
With sickness and disease thou bow'st them down,
Painful diseases and deformed,
In crude old age;
Though not disordinate, yet causeless suffering
The punishment of dissolute days; in fine,
Just or unjust alike seem miserable,
For oft alike both come to evil end.

(Lines 667–704)

*

Dal. Yet hear me, Samson; not that I endeavour
To lessen or extenuate my offence,
But that, on the other side, if it be weighed
By itself, with aggravations not surcharged,
Or else with just allowance counterpoised,
I may, if possible, thy pardon find
The easier towards me, or thy hatred less.
First granting, as I do, it was a weakness
In me, but incident to all our sex,
Curiosity, inquisitive, importune

Of secrets, then with like infirmity
To publish them – both common female faults –
Was it not weakness also to make known,
For importunity, that is for naught,
Wherein consisted all thy strength and safety?
To what I did thou show'dst me first the way.
But I to enemies revealed, and should not.
Nor should'st thou have trusted that to woman's frailty:
Ere I to thee, thou to thyself wast cruel.
Let weakness, then, with weakness come to parle,
So near related, or the same of kind;
Thine forgive mine, that men may censure thine
The gentler, if severely thou exact not
More strength from me than in thyself was found.
And what if love, which thou interpret'st hate,
The jealousy of love, powerful of sway
In human hearts, nor less in mine towards thee,
Caused what I did? I saw thee mutable
Of fancy; feared lest one day thou would'st leave me,
As her at Timna; sought by all means, therefore,
How to endear, and hold thee to me firmest:
No better way I saw than by importuning
To learn thy secrets, get into my power
Thy key of strength and safety; thou wilt say,
'Why, then, revealed?' I was assured by those
Who tempted me that nothing was designed
Against thee but safe custody and hold:

That made for me; I knew that liberty
Would draw thee forth to perilous enterprises,
While I at home sat full of cares and fears,
Wailing thy absence in my widowed bed;
Here I should still enjoy thee, day and night,
Mine and love's prisoner, not the Philistines',
Whole to myself, unhazarded abroad,
Fearless at home of partners in my love.
These reasons in love's law have passed for good,
Though fond and reasonless to some perhaps;
And love hath oft, well meaning, wrought much woe,
Yet always pity or pardon hath obtained.
Be not unlike all others, not austere
As thou art strong, inflexible as steel.
If thou in strength all mortals dost exceed,
In uncompassionate anger do not so.

(Lines 766–818)

*

 Chor. It is not virtue, wisdom, valour, wit,
Strength, comeliness of shape, or amplest merit
That woman's love can win, or long inherit;
But what it is, hard is to say,
Harder to hit,
(Which way soever men refer it) –
Much like thy riddle, Samson – in one day

Or seven though one should musing sit;
  If any of these, or all, the Timnian bride
Had not so soon preferred
Thy paranymph, worthless to thee compared,
Successor in thy bed,
Nor both so loosely disallied
Their nuptials, nor this last so treacherously
Had shorn the fatal harvest of thy head.
Is it for that such outward ornament
Was lavished on their sex, that inward gifts
Were left for haste unfinished, judgement scant,
Capacity not raised to apprehend
Or value what is best
In choice, but oftest to affect the wrong?
Or was too much of self-love mixed,
Of constancy no root infixed,
That either they love nothing, or not long?
  Whate'er it be, to wisest men and best,
Seeming at first all heavenly under virgin veil,
Soft, modest, meek, demure,
Once joined, the contrary she proves – a thorn
Intestine, far within defensive arms
A cleaving mischief, in his way to virtue
Adverse and turbulent; or by her charms
Draws him awry, enslaved
With dotage, and his sense depraved
To folly and shameful deeds, which ruin ends.

What pilot so expert but needs must wreck,
Embarked with such a steers-mate at the helm?
    Favoured of heaven who finds
One virtuous, rarely found,
That in domestic good combines:
Happy that house! His way to peace is smooth:
But virtue which breaks through all opposition,
And all temptation can remove,
Most shines and most is ácceptable above.
    Therefore God's universal law
Gave to the man despotic power
Over his female in due awe,
Nor from that right to part an hour,
Smile she or lour:
So shall he least confusion draw
On his whole life, not swayed
By female usurpation, not dismayed.

(Lines 1010–1060)

*

Messenger. Occasions drew me early to this city,
And, as the gates I entered with sun-rise,
The morning trumpets festival proclaimed
Through each high street; little I had dispatched,
When all abroad was rumoured that this day
Samson should be brought forth, to show the people

Proof of his mighty strength in feats and games;
I sorrowed at his captive state, but minded
Not to be absent at that spectacle.
The building was a spacious theatre,
Half round on two main pillars vaulted high,
With seats where all the lords, and each degree
Of sort, might sit in order to behold;
The other side was open, where the throng
On banks and scaffolds under sky might stand:
I among these aloof obscurely stood.
The feast and noon grew high, and sacrifice
Had filled their hearts with mirth, high cheer, and wine,
When to their sports they turned. Immediately
Was Samson as a public servant brought,
In their state livery clad: before him pipes
And timbrels; on each side went armed guards;
Both horse and foot before him and behind,
Archers and slingers, cataphracts and spears.
At sight of him the people with a shout
Rifted the air, clamouring their god with praise,
Who had made their dreadful enemy their thrall.
He patient, but undaunted, where they led him,
Came to the place; and what was set before him,
Which without help of eye might be assayed,
To heave, pull, draw, or break, he still performed
All with incredible, stupendous force,
None daring to appear antagonist.

At length, for intermission sake, they led him
Between the pillars; he his guide requested
(For so from such as nearer stood we heard),
As over-tired, to let him lean a while
With both his arms on those two massy pillars,
That to the arched roof gave main support.
He unsuspicious led him; which when Samson
Felt in his arms, with head a while inclined,
And eyes fast fixed, he stood, as one who prayed,
Or some great matter in his mind revolved.
At last, with head erect, thus cried aloud:
'Hitherto, Lords, what your commands imposed
I have performed, as reason was, obeying,
Not without wonder or delight beheld.
Now, of my own accord, such other trial
I mean to show you of my strength yet greater
As with amaze shall strike all who behold.'
This uttered, straining all his nerves, he bowed;
As with the force of winds and waters pent
When mountains tremble, those two massy pillars
With horrible convulsion to and fro
He tugged, he shook, till down they came, and drew
The whole roof after them with burst of thunder
Upon the heads of all who sat beneath,
Lords, ladies, captains, counsellors, or priests,
Their choice nobility and flower, not only
Of this, but each Philistian city round,

Met from all parts to solemnize this feast.
Samson, with these immixed, inevitably
Pulled down the same destruction on himself;
The vulgar only scaped, who stood without.
    Chor. O dearly bought revenge, yet glorious!
Living or dying thou hast fulfilled
The work for which thou wast foretold
To Israel, and now liest victorious
Among thy slain self-killed,
Not willingly, but tangled in the fold
Of dire Necessity, whose law in death conjoined
Thee with thy slaughtered foes, in number more
Than all thy life had slain before.
    Semichor. While their hearts were jocund and sublime,
Drunk with idolatry, drunk with wine
And fat regorged of bulls and goats,
Chanting their idol, and preferring
Before our living Dread, who dwells
In Silo, his bright sanctuary,
Among them he a spirit of frenzy sent,
Who hurt their minds,
And urged them on with mad desire
To call in haste for their destroyer;
They, only set on sport and play,
Unweetingly importuned
Their own destruction to come speedy upon them.
So fond are mortal men,

Fallen into wrath divine,
As their own ruin on themselves to invite,
Insensate left, or to sense reprobate,
And with blindness internal struck.

    Semichor. But he, though blind of sight,
Despised, and thought extinguished quite,
With inward eyes illuminated,
His fiery virtue roused
From under ashes into sudden flame,
And as an evening dragon came,
Assailant on the perched roosts
And nests in order ranged
Of tame villatic fowl; but as an eagle
His cloudless thunder bolted on their heads.
So Virtue, given for lost,
Depressed and overthrown, as seemed,
Like that self-begotten bird,
In the Arabian woods embossed,
That no second knows nor third,
And lay erewhile a holocaust,
From out her ashy womb now teemed,
Revives, reflourishes, then vigorous most
When most unactive deemed;
And, though her body die, her fame survives,
A secular bird, ages of lives.

    Man. Come, come; no time for lamentation now,
Nor much more cause: Samson hath quit himself

Like Samson, and heroicly hath finished
A life heroic, on his enemies
Fully revenged – hath left them years of mourning
And lamentation to the sons of Caphtor
Through all Philistian bounds; to Israel
Honour hath left and freedom, let but them
Find courage to lay hold on this occasion;
To himself and father's house eternal fame;
And, which is best and happiest yet, all this
With God not parted from him, as was feared,
But favouring and assisting to the end.
Nothing is here for tears, nothing to wail
Or knock the breast, no weakness, no contempt
Dispraise, or blame, nothing but well and fair,
And what may quiet us in a death so noble.
Let us go find the body where it lies
Soaked in his enemies' blood, and from the stream
With lavers pure, and cleansing herbs, wash off
The clotted gore. I, with what speed the while
(Gaza is not in plight to say us nay)
Will send for all my kindred, all my friends,
To fetch him hence, and solemnly attend,
With silent obsequy and funeral train,
Home to his father's house; there will I build him
A monument, and plant it round with shade
Of laurel ever green and branching palm,
With all his trophies hung, and acts enrolled

In copious legend, or sweet lyric song;
Thither shall all the valiant youth resort,
And from his memory inflame their breasts
To matchless valour and adventures high;
The virgins also shall, on feastful days,
Visit his tomb with flowers, only bewailing
His lot unfortunate in nuptial choice,
From whence captivity and loss of eyes.

    Chor. All is best, though we oft doubt
What the unsearchable dispose
Of highest Wisdom brings about,
And ever best found in the close.
Oft he seems to hide his face,
But unexpectedly returns,
And to his faithful champion hath in place
Bore witness gloriously; whence Gaza mourns,
And all that band them to resist
His uncontrollable intent;
His servants he, with new acquist
Of true experience from this great event,
With peace and consolation hath dismissed,
And calm of mind, all passion spent.

                  (Lines 1596–1758)

From
PARADISE LOST

THE PRINTER TO THE READER

Courteous reader, there was no argument at first intended to the book, but for the satisfaction of many that have desired it, I have procured it, and withal a reason of that which stumbled many others: why the poem rhymes not.

S. Simmons

The measure is English heroic verse without rhyme, as that of Homer in Greek, and of Virgil in Latin – rhyme being no necessary adjunct or true ornament of poem or good verse, in longer works especially, but the invention of a barbarous age, to set off wretched matter and lame metre; graced indeed since by the use of some famous modern poets, carried away by custom, but much to their own vexation, hindrance, and constraint to express many things otherwise, and for the most part worse, than else they would have expressed them. Not without cause therefore some both Italian and Spanish poets of prime note have rejected rhyme both in longer and shorter works, as have also long since our best English tragedies, as a thing of itself, to all judicious ears, trivial and of no true musical delight; which consists only in apt numbers, fit quantity of syllables, and the sense variously drawn out from one verse into another, not in the jingling sound of like endings – a fault avoided by the learned ancients both in poetry and all good oratory. This neglect then of rhyme so little is to be taken for a defect, though it may seem so perhaps to vulgar readers, that it rather is to be esteemed an example set, the first in English, of ancient liberty recovered to heroic poem from the troublesome and modern bondage of rhyming.

BOOK I

THE ARGUMENT

This first book proposes, first in brief, the whole subject
– man's disobedience, and the loss thereupon of Para-
dise, wherein he was placed: then touches the prime
cause of his fall – the serpent, or rather Satan in the
serpent; who, revolting from God, and drawing to his
side many legions of angels, was, by the command of
God, driven out of heaven, with all his crew, into the
great deep. Which action passed over, the poem hastens
into the midst of things; presenting Satan, with his
angels, now fallen into hell – described here not in the
centre (for heaven and earth may be supposed as yet not
made, certainly not yet accursed) but in a place of utter
darkness, fitliest called Chaos. Here Satan, with his
angels lying on the burning lake, thunderstruck and
astonished, after a certain space recovers, as from con-
fusion; calls up him who, next in order and dignity, lay
by him; they confer of their miserable fall. Satan awakens
all his legions, who lay till then in the same manner
confounded; they rise: their numbers; array of battle;
their chief leaders named, according to the idols known
afterwards in Canaan and the countries adjoining. To
these Satan directs his speech; comforts them with hope
yet of regaining heaven; but tells them, lastly, of a new
world and new kind of creature to be created, according

to an ancient prophecy, or report, in heaven – for that
angels were long before this visible creation was the
opinion of many ancient fathers. To find out the truth
of this prophecy, and what to determine thereon, he
refers to a full council. What his associates thence
attempt. Pandemonium, the palace of Satan, rises, sud-
denly built out of the deep: the infernal peers there sit
in council.

Of man's first disobedience, and the fruit
Of that forbidden tree whose mortal taste
Brought death into the world, and all our woe,
With loss of Eden, till one greater man
Restore us, and regain the blissful seat,
Sing, heavenly Muse, that, on the secret top
Of Oreb, or of Sinai, didst inspire
That shepherd who first taught the chosen seed
In the beginning how the heavens and earth
Rose out of chaos: or, if Zion hill
Delight thee more, and Siloa's brook that flowed
Fast by the oracle of God, I thence
Invoke thy aid to my adventurous song,
That with no middle flight intends to soar
Above the Aonian mount, while it pursues
Things unattempted yet in prose or rhyme.
And chiefly thou, O Spirit, that dost prefer
Before all temples the upright heart and pure,

Instruct me, for thou know'st; thou from the first
Wast present, and, with mighty wings outspread
Dove-like sat'st brooding on the vast abyss,
And mad'st it pregnant: what in me is dark
Illumine, what is low raise and support:
That, to the height of this great argument,
I may assert eternal providence,
And justify the ways of God to men.

　　Say first – for heaven hides nothing from thy view,
Nor the deep tract of hell – say first what cause
Moved our grand parents, in that happy state,
Favoured of heaven so highly, to fall off
From their creator, and transgress his will
For one restraint, lords of the world besides.
Who first seduced them to that foul revolt?

　　The infernal serpent; he it was whose guile,
Stirred up with envy and revenge, deceived
The mother of mankind, what time his pride
Had cast him out from heaven, with all his host
Of rebel angels, by whose aid, aspiring
To set himself in glory above his peers,
He trusted to have equalled the most high,
If he opposed, and, with ambitious aim
Against the throne and monarchy of God,
Raised impious war in heaven and battle proud,
With vain attempt. Him the almighty power
Hurled headlong flaming from the ethereal sky,

With hideous ruin and combustion, down
To bottomless perdition, there to dwell
In adamantine chains and penal fire,
Who durst defy the omnipotent to arms.
   Nine times the space that measures day and night
To mortal men, he with his horrid crew
Lay vanquished, rolling in the fiery gulf,
Confounded, though immortal: but his doom
Reserved him to more wrath; for now the thought
Both of lost happiness and lasting pain
Torments him; round he throws his baleful eyes,
That witnessed huge affliction and dismay,
Mixed with obdurate pride and steadfast hate;
At once, as far as angels ken, he views
The dismal situation waste and wild:
A dungeon horrible, on all sides round,
As one great furnace flamed, yet from those flames
No light, but rather darkness visible
Served only to discover sights of woe,
Regions of sorrow, doleful shades, where peace
And rest can never dwell, hope never comes
That comes to all, but torture without end
Still urges, and a fiery deluge, fed
With ever-burning sulphur unconsumed:
Such place eternal justice had prepared
For those rebellious; here their prison ordained
In utter darkness, and their portion set,

As far removed from God and light of heaven
As from the centre thrice to the utmost pole.
O how unlike the place from whence they fell!
There the companions of his fall, o'erwhelmed
With floods and whirlwinds of tempestuous fire,
He soon discerns; and weltering by his side,
One next himself in power, and next in crime,
Long after known in Palestine, and named
Beëlzebub. To whom the arch-enemy,
And thence in heaven called Satan, with bold words
Breaking the horrid silence, thus began:
    'If thou beest he – but O how fallen! How changed
From him, who in the happy realms of light,
Clothed with transcendent brightness, didst outshine
Myriads, though bright – if he whom mutual league,
United thoughts and counsels, equal hope
And hazard in the glorious enterprise,
Joined with me once, now misery hath joined
In equal ruin; into what pit thou seest
From what height fallen: so much the stronger proved
He with his thunder: and till then who knew
The force of those dire arms? Yet not for those,
Nor what the potent victor in his rage
Can else inflict, do I repent, or change,
Though changed in outward lustre, that fixed mind,
And high disdain from sense of injured merit,
That with the mightiest raised me to contend,

And to the fierce contentions brought along
Innumerable force of spirits armed,
That durst dislike his reign, and, me preferring,
His utmost power with adverse power opposed
In dubious battle on the plains of heaven,
And shook his throne. What though the field be lost?
All is not lost – the unconquerable will,
And study of revenge, immortal hate,
And courage never to submit or yield:
And what is else not to be overcome?
That glory never shall his wrath or might
Extort from me. To bow and sue for grace
With suppliant knee, and deify his power
Who, from the terror of this arm, so late
Doubted his empire – that were low indeed;
That were an ignominy and shame beneath
This downfall; since, by fate, the strength of gods,
And this empyreal substance, cannot fail;
Since, through experience of this great event,
In arms not worse, in foresight much advanced,
We may with more successful hope resolve
To wage by force or guile eternal war,
Irreconcilable to our grand foe,
Who now triumphs, and in the excess of joy
Sole reigning holds the tyranny of heaven.'
    So spake the apostate angel, though in pain,
Vaunting aloud, but racked with deep despair;

And him thus answered soon his bold compeer:
  'O Prince, O chief of many thronèd powers
That led the embattled seraphim to war
Under thy conduct, and in dreadful deeds
Fearless, endangered heaven's perpetual king,
And put to proof his high supremacy,
Whether upheld by strength, or chance, or fate,
Too well I see and rue the dire event
That, with sad overthrow and foul defeat,
Hath lost us heaven, and all this mighty host
In horrible destruction laid thus low,
As far as gods and heavenly essences
Can perish: for the mind and spirit remains
Invincible, and vigour soon returns,
Though all our glory extinct, and happy state
Here swallowed up in endless misery.
But what if he our conqueror (whom I now
Of force believe almighty, since no less
Than such could have o'erpowered such force as ours)
Have left us this our spirit and strength entire,
Strongly to suffer and support our pains,
That we may so suffice his vengeful ire,
Or do him mightier service as his thralls
By right of war, whate'er his business be,
Here in the heart of hell to work in fire,
Or do his errands in the gloomy deep?
What can it then avail though yet we feel

Strength undiminished, or eternal being
To undergo eternal punishment?'
    Whereto with speedy words the arch-fiend replied:
'Fallen cherub, to be weak is miserable,
Doing or suffering: but of this be sure –
To do aught good never will be our task,
But ever to do ill our sole delight,
As being the contrary to his high will
Whom we resist. If then his providence
Out of our evil seek to bring forth good,
Our labour must be to pervert that end,
And out of good still to find means of evil;
Which ofttimes may succeed so as perhaps
Shall grieve him, if I fail not, and disturb
His inmost counsels from their destined aim.
But see, the angry victor hath recalled
His ministers of vengeance and pursuit
Back to the gates of heaven: the sulphurous hail,
Shot after us in storm, o'erblown hath laid
The fiery surge that from the precipice
Of heaven received us falling; and the thunder,
Winged with red lightning and impetuous rage,
Perhaps hath spent his shafts, and ceases now
To bellow through the vast and boundless deep.
Let us not slip the occasion, whether scorn
Or satiate fury yield it from our foe.
Seest thou yon dreary plain, forlorn and wild,

The seat of desolation, void of light,
Save what the glimmering of these livid flames
Casts pale and dreadful? Thither let us tend
From off the tossing of these fiery waves;
There rest, if any rest can harbour there;
And, re-assembling our afflicted powers,
Consult how we may henceforth most offend
Our enemy, our own loss how repair,
How overcome this dire calamity,
What reinforcement we may gain from hope,
If not, what resolution from despair.'

   Thus Satan, talking to his nearest mate,
With head uplift above the wave, and eyes
That sparkling blazed; his other parts besides
Prone on the flood, extended long and large,
Lay floating many a rood, in bulk as huge
As whom the fables name of monstrous size,
Titanian or Earth-born, that warred on Jove,
Briareos or Typhon, whom the den
By ancient Tarsus held, or that sea-beast
Leviathan, which God of all his works
Created hugest that swim the ocean stream;
Him, haply slumbering on the Norway foam,
The pilot of some small night-foundered skiff,
Deeming some island, oft, as seamen tell,
With fixèd anchor in his scaly rind,
Moors by his side under the lee, while night

Invests the sea, and wishèd morn delays;
So stretched out huge in length the arch-fiend lay,
Chained on the burning lake; nor ever thence
Had risen, or heaved his head, but that the will
And high permission of all-ruling heaven
Left him at large to his own dark designs,
That with reiterated crimes he might
Heap on himself damnation, while he sought
Evil to others, and enraged might see
How all his malice served but to bring forth
Infinite goodness, grace and mercy, shown
On man by him seduced, but on himself
Treble confusion, wrath, and vengeance poured.

   Forthwith upright he rears from off the pool
His mighty stature; on each hand the flames
Driven backward slope their pointing spires, and, rolled
In billows, leave i' the midst a horrid vale.
Then with expanded wings he steers his flight
Aloft, incumbent on the dusky air,
That felt unusual weight; till on dry land
He lights – if it were land that ever burned
With solid, as the lake with liquid fire,
And such appeared in hue as when the force
Of subterranean wind transports a hill
Torn from Pelorus, or the shattered side
Of thundering Etna, whose combustible
And fuelled entrails, thence conceiving fire,

Sublimed with mineral fury, aid the winds,
And leave a singèd bottom all involved
With stench and smoke: such resting found the sole
Of unblessed feet. Him followed his next mate,
Both glorying to have scaped the Stygian flood
As gods, and by their own recovered strength,
Not by the sufferance of supernal power.

'Is this the region, this the soil, the clime,'
Said then the lost archangel, 'this the seat
That we must change for heaven, this mournful gloom
For that celestial light? Be it so, since he
Who now is sovereign can dispose and bid
What shall be right: farthest from him is best,
Whom reason hath equalled, force hath made supreme
Above his equals. Farewell, happy fields,
Where joy for ever dwells; hail, horrors, hail,
Infernal world; and thou, profoundest hell,
Receive thy new possessor – one who brings
A mind not to be changed by place or time.
The mind is its own place, and in itself
Can make a heaven of hell, a hell of heaven.
What matter where, if I be still the same,
And what I should be, all, but less than he
Whom thunder hath made greater? Here at least
We shall be free; the almighty hath not built
Here for his envy, will not drive us hence:
Here we may reign secure; and, in my choice,

To reign is worth ambition, though in hell:
Better to reign in hell than serve in heaven.
But wherefore let we then our faithful friends,
The associates and co-partners of our loss,
Lie thus astonished on the oblivious pool,
And call them not to share with us their part
In this unhappy mansion, or once more
With rallied arms to try what may be yet
Regained in heaven, or what more lost in hell?'

   So Satan spake, and him Beëlzebub
Thus answered: 'Leader of those armies bright
Which, but the omnipotent, none could have foiled;
If once they hear that voice, their liveliest pledge
Of hope in fears and dangers – heard so oft
In worst extremes, and on the perilous edge
Of battle, when it raged, in all assaults
Their surest signal – they will soon resume
New courage and revive, though now they lie
Grovelling and prostrate on yon lake of fire,
As we erewhile, astounded and amazed;
No wonder, fallen such a pernicious height.'

   He scarce had ceased when the superior fiend
Was moving toward the shore; his ponderous shield,
Ethereal temper, massy, large, and round,
Behind him cast; the broad circumference
Hung on his shoulders like the moon, whose orb
Through optic glass the Tuscan artist views

At evening, from the top of Fesolè,
Or in Valdarno, to descry new lands,
Rivers, or mountains, in her spotty globe.
His spear – to equal which the tallest pine
Hewn on Norwegian hills, to be the mast
Of some great ammiral, were but a wand –
He walked with, to support uneasy steps
Over the burning marl, not like those steps
On heaven's azure; and the torrid clime
Smote on him sore besides, vaulted with fire;
Nathless he so endured, till on the beach
Of that inflamèd sea he stood, and called
His legions – angel forms, who lay entranced
Thick as autumnal leaves that strew the brooks
In Vallombrosa, where the Etrurian shades
High over-arched embower; or scattered sedge
Afloat, when with fierce winds Orion armed
Hath vexed the Red Sea coast, whose waves o'erthrew
Busiris and his Memphian chivalry,
While with perfidious hatred they pursued
The sojourners of Goshen, who beheld
From the safe shore their floating carcasses
And broken chariot-wheels: so thick bestrewn,
Abject and lost, lay these, covering the flood,
Under amazement of their hideous change.
He called so loud that all the hollow deep
Of hell resounded: 'Princes, potentates,

Warriors, the flower of heaven – once yours; now lost,
If such astonishment as this can seize
Eternal spirits; or have ye chosen this place
After the toil of battle to repose
Your wearied virtue, for the ease you find
To slumber here, as in the vales of heaven?
Or in this abject posture have ye sworn
To adore the conqueror, who now beholds
Cherub and seraph rolling in the flood
With scattered arms and ensigns, till anon
His swift pursuers from heaven-gates discern
The advantage, and, descending, tread us down
Thus drooping, or with linkèd thunderbolts
Transfix us to the bottom of this gulf?
Awake, arise, or be for ever fallen.'

(Lines 1–330)

*

Say, Muse, their names then known, who first,
    who last,
Roused from the slumber on that fiery couch,
At their great emperor's call, as next in worth
Came singly where he stood on the bare strand,
While the promiscuous crowd stood yet aloof.
    The chief were those who, from the pit of hell
Roaming to seek their prey on earth, durst fix

Their seats, long after, next the seat of God,
Their altars by his altar, gods adored
Among the nations round, and durst abide
Jehovah thundering out of Zion, throned
Between the cherubim; yea, often placed
Within his sanctuary itself their shrines,
Abominations; and with cursed things
His holy rites and solemn feasts profaned,
And with their darkness durst affront his light.
First, Moloch, horrid king, besmeared with blood
Of human sacrifice, and parents' tears;
Though for the noise of drums and timbrels loud,
Their children's cries unheard that passed through fire
To his grim idol. Him the Ammonite
Worshipped in Rabba and her watery plain,
In Argob and in Basan, to the stream
Of utmost Arnon. Nor content with such
Audacious neighbourhood, the wisest heart
Of Solomon he led by fraud to build
His temple right against the temple of God
On that opprobrious hill, and made his grove
The pleasant valley of Hinnom, Tophet thence
And black Gehenna called, the type of hell.
Next Chemos, the obscene dread of Moab's sons,
From Aroer to Nebo and the wild
Of southmost Abarim; in Hesebon
And Horonaim, Seon's realm, beyond

The flowery dale of Sibma clad with vines,
And Elealè to the Asphaltic Pool:
Peor his other name, when he enticed
Israel in Sittim, on their march from Nile,
To do him wanton rites, which cost them woe.
Yet thence his lustful orgies he enlarged
Even to that hill of scandal, by the grove
Of Moloch homicide, lust hard by hate,
Till good Josiah drove them thence to hell.
With these came they who, from the bordering flood
Of old Euphrates to the brook that parts
Egypt from Syrian ground, had general names
Of Baälim and Ashtaroth – those male,
These feminine. For spirits, when they please,
Can either sex assume, or both; so oft
And uncompounded is their essence pure,
Not tied or manacled with joint or limb,
Nor founded on the brittle strength of bones,
Like cumbrous flesh; but in what shape they choose,
Dilated or condensed, bright or obscure,
Can execute their airy purposes,
And works of love or enmity fulfil.
For those the race of Israel oft forsook
Their living strength, and unfrequented left
His righteous altar, bowing lowly down
To bestial gods; for which their heads, as low
Bowed down in battle, sunk before the spear

Of despicable foes. With these in troop
Came Ashtoreth, whom the Phoenicians called
Astarte, queen of heaven, with crescent horns;
To whose bright image nightly by the moon
Sidonian virgins paid their vows and songs;
In Zion also not unsung, where stood
Her temple on the offensive mountain, built
By that uxorious king whose heart, though large,
Beguiled by fair idolatresses, fell
To idols foul. Thammuz came next behind,
Whose annual wound in Lebanon allured
The Syrian damsels to lament his fate
In amorous ditties all a summer's day,
While smooth Adonis from his native rock
Ran purple to the sea, supposed with blood
Of Thammuz yearly wounded: the love-tale
Infected Zion's daughters with like heat,
Whose wanton passions in the sacred porch
Ezekiel saw, when by the vision led
His eye surveyed the dark idolatries
Of alienated Judah. Next came one
Who mourned in earnest, when the captive ark
Maimed his brute image, head and hands lopped off,
In his own temple, on the groundsel edge,
Where he fell flat and shamed his worshippers:
Dagon his name, sea-monster, upward man
And downward fish; yet had his temple high

Reared in Azotus, dreaded through the coast
Of Palestine, in Gath and Ascalon,
And Accaron and Gaza's frontier bounds.
Him followed Rimmon, whose delightful seat
Was fair Damascus, on the fertile banks
Of Abbana and Pharphar, lucid streams.
He also against the house of God was bold:
A leper once he lost, and gained a king –
Ahaz, his sottish conqueror, whom he drew
God's altar to disparage and displace
For one of Syrian mode, whereon to burn
His odious offerings, and adore the gods
Whom he had vanquished. After these appeared
A crew who, under names of old renown –
Osiris, Isis, Orus, and their train –
With monstrous shapes and sorceries abused
Fanatic Egypt and her priests to seek
Their wandering gods disguised in brutish forms
Rather than human. Nor did Israel scape
The infection, when their borrowed gold composed
The calf in Oreb; and the rebel king
Doubled that sin in Bethel and in Dan,
Likening his maker to the grazèd ox –
Jehovah, who, in one night, when he passed
From Egypt marching, equalled with one stroke
Both her first-born and all her bleating gods.
Belial came last; than whom a spirit more lewd

Fell not from heaven, or more gross to love
Vice for itself: to him no temple stood
Or altar smoked; yet who more oft than he
In temples and at altars, when the priest
Turns atheist, as did Eli's sons, who filled
With lust and violence the house of God?
In courts and palaces he also reigns,
And in luxurious cities, where the noise
Of riot ascends above their loftiest towers,
And injury and outrage; and when night
Darkens the streets, then wander forth the sons
Of Belial, flown with insolence and wine.
Witness the streets of Sodom, and that night
In Gibeah, when the hospitable door
Exposed a matron, to avoid worse rape.

(Lines 376–505)

*

All these and more came flocking; but with looks
Downcast and damp; yet such wherein appeared
Obscure some glimpse of joy to have found their chief
Not in despair, to have found themselves not lost
In loss itself; which on his countenance cast
Like doubtful hue; but he, his wonted pride
Soon recollecting, with high words, that bore
Semblance of worth, not substance, gently raised

Their fainting courage, and dispelled their fears.
Then straight commands that, at the warlike sound
Of trumpets loud and clarions, be upreared
His mighty standard; that proud honour claimed
Azazel as his right, a cherub tall:
Who forthwith from the glittering staff unfurled
The imperial ensign, which, full high advanced,
Shone like a meteor streaming to the wind,
With gems and golden lustre rich emblazed,
Seraphic arms and trophies; all the while
Sonorous metal blowing martial sounds:
At which the universal host upsent
A shout that tore hell's concave, and beyond
Frighted the reign of Chaos and old Night.
All in a moment through the gloom were seen
Ten thousand banners rise into the air,
With orient colours waving: with them rose
A forest huge of spears; and thronging helms
Appeared, and serried shields in thick array
Of depth immeasurable; anon they move
In perfect phalanx to the Dorian mood
Of flutes and soft recorders – such as raised
To height of noblest temper heroes old
Arming to battle, and instead of rage
Deliberate valour breathed, firm and unmoved
With dread of death to flight or foul retreat;
Nor wanting power to mitigate and swage

With solemn touches troubled thoughts, and chase
Anguish and doubt and fear and sorrow and pain
From mortal or immortal minds. Thus they,
Breathing united force with fixèd thought,
Moved on in silence to soft pipes that charmed
Their painful steps o'er the burnt soil; and now
Advanced in view they stand – a horrid front
Of dreadful length and dazzling arms, in guise
Of warriors old, with ordered spear and shield,
Awaiting what command their mighty chief
Had to impose: he through the armèd files
Darts his experienced eye, and soon traverse
The whole battalion views – their order due,
Their visages and stature as of gods;
Their number last he sums. And now his heart
Distends with pride, and, hardening in his strength,
Glories: for never, since created man,
Met such embodied force as, named with these,
Could merit more than that small infantry
Warred on by cranes – though all the giant brood
Of Phlegra with the heroic race were joined
That fought at Thebes and Ilium, on each side
Mixed with auxiliar gods; and what resounds
In fable or romance of Uther's son,
Begirt with British and Armoric knights;
And all who since, baptized or infidel,
Jousted in Aspramont, or Montalban,

Damasco, or Marocco, or Trebizond,
Or whom Bizerta sent from Afric shore
When Charlemagne with all his peerage fell
By Fontarabbia. Thus far these beyond
Compare of mortal prowess, yet observed
Their dread commander; he above the rest
In shape and gesture proudly eminent,
Stood like a tower; his form had yet not lost
All her original brightness, nor appeared
Less than archangel ruined, and the excess
Of glory obscured: as when the sun new risen
Looks through the horizontal misty air
Shorn of his beams, or from behind the moon
In dim eclipse, disastrous twilight sheds
On half the nations, and with fear of change
Perplexes monarchs. Darkened so, yet shone
Above them all the archangel: but his face
Deep scars of thunder had intrenched, and care
Sat on his faded cheek, but under brows
Of dauntless courage, and considerate pride
Waiting revenge; cruel his eye, but cast
Signs of remorse and passion, to behold
The fellows of his crime, the followers rather
(Far other once beheld in bliss), condemned
For ever now to have their lot in pain —
Millions of spirits for his fault amerced
Of heaven, and from eternal splendours flung

For his revolt – yet faithful how they stood,
Their glory withered; as, when heaven's fire
Hath scathed the forest oaks or mountain pines,
With singèd top their stately growth, though bare,
Stands on the blasted heath. He now prepared
To speak; whereat their doubled ranks they bend
From wing to wing, and half enclose him round
With all his peers: attention held them mute.
Thrice he assayed, and thrice, in spite of scorn,
Tears, such as angels weep, burst forth: at last
Words interwove with sighs found out their way.

　'O myriads of immortal spirits, O powers
Matchless, but with the Almighty – and that strife
Was not inglorious, though the event was dire,
As this place testifies, and this dire change,
Hateful to utter; but what power of mind,
Foreseeing or presaging, from the depth
Of knowledge past or present, could have feared
How such united force of gods, how such
As stood like these, could ever know repulse?
For who can yet believe, though after loss,
That all these puissant legions, whose exile
Hath emptied heaven, shall fail to re-ascend,
Self-raised, and repossess their native seat?
For me be witness all the host of heaven
If counsels different, or danger shunned
By me, have lost our hopes. But he who reigns

Monarch in heaven, till then as one secure
Sat on his throne, upheld by old repute,
Consent or custom, and his regal state
Put forth at full, but still his strength concealed –
Which tempted our attempt, and wrought our fall.
Henceforth his might we know, and know our own,
So as not either to provoke, or dread
New war provoked: our better part remains
To work in close design, by fraud or guile,
What force effected not; that he no less
At length from us may find, who overcomes
By force hath overcome but half his foe.
Space may produce new worlds; whereof so rife
There went a flame in heaven that he ere long
Intended to create, and therein plant
A generation whom his choice regard
Should favour equal to the sons of heaven.
Thither, if but to pry, shall be perhaps
Our first eruption – thither, or elsewhere;
For this infernal pit shall never hold
Celestial spirits in bondage, nor the abyss
Long under darkness cover. But these thoughts
Full counsel must mature; peace is despaired,
For who can think submission? War, then, war
Open or understood, must be resolved.'

(Lines 522–662)

Meanwhile the wingèd heralds, by command
Of sovereign power, with awful ceremony
And trumpet's sound, throughout the host proclaim
A solemn council forthwith to be held
At Pandemonium, the high capital
Of Satan and his peers; their summons called
From every band and squarèd regiment
By place or choice the worthiest; they anon
With hundreds and with thousands trooping came
Attended; all access was thronged; the gates
And porches wide, but chief the spacious hall
(Though like a covered field, where champions bold
Wont ride in armed, and at the soldan's chair
Defied the best of paynim chivalry
To mortal combat, or career with lance),
Thick swarmed, both on the ground and in the air,
Brushed with the hiss of rustling wings. As bees
In spring-time, when the sun with Taurus rides,
Pour forth their populous youth about the hive
In clusters; they among fresh dews and flowers
Fly to and fro, or on the smoothèd plank,
The suburb of their straw-built citadel,
New rubbed with balm, expatiate, and confer
Their state-affairs: so thick the airy crowd
Swarmed and were straitened; till, the signal given
Behold a wonder! They but now who seemed
In bigness to surpass Earth's giant sons,

Now less than smallest dwarfs, in narrow room
Throng numberless – like that pygmean race
Beyond the Indian mount, or fairy elves,
Whose midnight revels, by a forest side
Or fountain, some belated peasant sees,
Or dreams he sees, while overhead the moon
Sits arbitress, and nearer to the earth
Wheels her pale course: they, on their mirth and dance
Intent, with jocund music charm his ear;
At once with joy and fear his heart rebounds.
Thus incorporeal spirits to smallest forms
Reduced their shapes immense, and were at large,
Though without number still amidst the hall
Of that infernal court. But far within,
And in their own dimensions like themselves,
The great seraphic lords and cherubim
In close recess and secret conclave sat,
A thousand demi-gods on golden seats,
Frequent and full. After short silence then,
And summons read, the great consult began.

(Lines 752–798)

BOOK II

THE ARGUMENT

The consultation begun, Satan debates whether another battle be to be hazarded for the recovery of heaven: some advise it, others dissuade; a third proposal is preferred, mentioned before by Satan – to search the truth of that prophecy or tradition in heaven concerning another world, and another kind of creature, equal, or not much inferior, to themselves, about this time to be created; their doubt who shall be sent on this difficult search: Satan, their chief, undertakes alone the voyage; is honoured and applauded. The council thus ended, the rest betake them several ways and to several employments, as their inclinations lead them, to entertain the time till Satan return. He passes on his journey to hell gates, finds them shut, and who sat there to guard them; by whom at length they are opened, and discover to him the great gulf between hell and heaven. With what difficulty he passes through, directed by Chaos, the power of that place, to the sight of this new world which he sought.

High on a throne of royal state, which far
Outshone the wealth of Ormus and of Ind,
Or where the gorgeous East with richest hand
Showers on her kings barbaric pearl and gold,
Satan exalted sat, by merit raised
To that bad eminence; and, from despair
Thus high uplifted beyond hope, aspires
Beyond thus high, insatiate to pursue
Vain war with heaven; and, by success untaught,
His proud imaginations thus displayed:
    'Powers and dominions, deities of heaven –
For since no deep within her gulf can hold
Immortal vigour, though oppressed and fallen,
I give not heaven for lost. From this descent
Celestial virtues rising will appear
More glorious and more dread than from no fall,
And trust themselves to fear no second fate –
Me though just right, and the fixed laws of heaven,
Did first create your leader – next, free choice,
With what besides in council or in fight
Hath been achieved of merit – yet this loss,
Thus far at least recovered, hath much more
Established in a safe unenvied throne,
Yielded with full consent. The happier state
In heaven, which follows dignity, might draw
Envy from each inferior; but who here
Will envy whom the highest place exposes

Foremost to stand against the thunderer's aim
Your bulwark, and condemns to greatest share
Of endless pain? Where there is, then, no good
For which to strive, no strife can grow up there
From faction: for none sure will claim in hell
Precedence; none whose portion is so small
Of present pain that with ambitious mind
Will covet more. With this advantage, then,
To union, and firm faith, and firm accord,
More than can be in heaven, we now return
To claim our just inheritance of old,
Surer to prosper than prosperity
Could have assured us; and by what best way,
Whether of open war or covert guile,
We now debate: who can advise may speak.'

He ceased; and next him Moloch, sceptred king,
Stood up – the strongest and the fiercest spirit
That fought in heaven, now fiercer by despair
His trust was with the eternal to be deemed
Equal in strength, and rather than be less
Cared not to be at all; with that care lost
Went all his fear: of God, or hell, or worse,
He recked not, and these words thereafter spake:

'My sentence is for open war; of wiles,
More unexpert, I boast not: them let those
Contrive who need, or when they need; not now.
For while they sit contriving, shall the rest –

Millions that stand in arms, and longing wait
The signal to ascend – sit lingering here,
Heaven's fugitives, and for their dwelling place
Accept this dark opprobrious den of shame,
The prison of his tyranny who reigns
By our delay? No, let us rather choose,
Armed with hell flames and fury all at once
O'er heaven's high towers to force resistless way,
Turning our tortures into horrid arms
Against the torturer; when to meet the noise
Of his almighty engine, he shall hear
Infernal thunder, and for lightning see
Black fire and horror shot with equal rage
Among his angels, and his throne itself
Mixed with Tartarean sulphur and strange fire,
His own invented torments. But perhaps
The way seems difficult, and steep to scale
With upright wing against a higher foe.
Let such bethink them, if the sleepy drench
Of that forgetful lake benumb not still,
That in our proper motion we ascend
Up to our native seat; descent and fall
To us is adverse. Who but felt of late,
When the fierce foe hung on our broken rear
Insulting, and pursued us through the deep,
With what compulsion and laborious flight
We sunk thus low? The ascent is easy, then;

The event is feared; should we again provoke
Our stronger, some worse way his wrath may find
To our destruction, if there be in hell
Fear to be worse destroyed; what can be worse
Than to dwell here, driven out from bliss, condemned
In this abhorrèd deep to utter woe;
Where pain of unextinguishable fire
Must exercise us without hope of end
The vassals of his anger, when the scourge
Inexorably, and the torturing hour,
Calls us to penance? More destroyed than thus,
We should be quite abolished, and expire.
What fear we then? What doubt we to incense
His utmost ire? Which, to the height enraged,
Will either quite consume us, and reduce
To nothing this essential – happier far
Than miserable to have eternal being –
Or, if our substance be indeed divine,
And cannot cease to be, we are at worst
On this side nothing; and by proof we feel
Our power sufficient to disturb his heaven,
And with perpetual inroads to alarm,
Though inaccessible, his fatal throne:
Which, if not victory, is yet revenge.'

  He ended frowning, and his look denounced
Desperate revenge, and battle dangerous
To less than gods. On the other side up rose

Belial, in act more graceful and humane;
A fairer person lost not heaven; he seemed
For dignity composed, and high exploit:
But all was false and hollow; though his tongue
Dropped manna, and could make the worse appear
The better reason, to perplex and dash
Maturest counsels: for his thoughts were low –
To vice industrious, but to nobler deeds
Timorous and slothful; yet he pleased the ear,
And with persuasive accent thus began:
  'I should be much for open war, O peers,
As not behind in hate, if what was urged
Main reason to persuade immediate war
Did not dissuade me most, and seem to cast
Ominous conjecture on the whole success;
When he who most excels in fact of arms,
In what he counsels and in what excels
Mistrustful, grounds his courage on despair
And utter dissolution, as the scope
Of all his aim, after some dire revenge.
First, what revenge? The towers of heaven are filled
With armèd watch, that render all access
Impregnable: oft on the bordering deep
Encamp their legions, or with obscure wing
Scout far and wide into the realm of night,
Scorning surprise. Or could we break our way
By force, and at our heels all hell should rise

With blackest insurrection to confound
Heaven's purest light, yet our great enemy,
All incorruptible, would on his throne
Sit unpolluted, and the ethereal mould,
Incapable of stain, would soon expel
Her mischief, and purge off the baser fire,
Victorious. Thus repulsed, our final hope
Is flat despair: we must exasperate
The almighty victor to spend all his rage,
And that must end us, that must be our cure –
To be no more; sad cure; for who would lose,
Though full of pain, this intellectual being,
Those thoughts that wander through eternity,
To perish rather, swallowed up and lost
In the wide womb of uncreated night,
Devoid of sense and motion? And who knows,
Let this be good, whether our angry foe
Can give it, or will ever? How he can
Is doubtful; that he never will is sure.
Will he, so wise, let loose at once his ire,
Belike through impotence or unaware,
To give his enemies their wish, and end
Them in his anger whom his anger saves
To punish endless? "Wherefore cease we, then?"
Say they who counsel war; "we are decreed,
Reserved, and destined to eternal woe;
Whatever doing, what can we suffer more,

What can we suffer worse?" Is this, then, worst —
Thus sitting, thus consulting, thus in arms?
What when we fled amain, pursued and struck
With heaven's afflicting thunder, and besought
The deep to shelter us? This hell then seemed
A refuge from those wounds; or when we lay
Chained on the burning lake? That sure was worse.
What if the breath that kindled those grim fires,
Awaked, should blow them into sevenfold rage,
And plunge us in the flames? Or from above
Should intermitted vengeance arm again
His red right hand to plague us? What if all
Her stores were opened, and this firmament
Of hell should spout her cataracts of fire,
Impendent horrors, threatening hideous fall
One day upon our heads; while we perhaps,
Designing or exhorting glorious war,
Caught in a fiery tempest, shall be hurled,
Each on his rock transfixed, the sport and prey
Of racking whirlwinds, or for ever sunk
Under yon boiling ocean, wrapped in chains,
There to converse with everlasting groans,
Unrespited, unpitied, unreprieved,
Ages of hopeless end? This would be worse.
War, therefore, open or concealed, alike
My voice dissuades; for what can force or guile
With him, or who deceive his mind, whose eye

Views all things at one view? He from heaven's height
All these our motions vain sees and derides,
Not more almighty to resist our might
Than wise to frustrate all our plots and wiles.
Shall we, then, live thus vile – the race of heaven
Thus trampled, thus expelled, to suffer here
Chains and these torments? Better these than worse,
By my advice; since fate inevitable
Subdues us, and omnipotent decree,
The victor's will. To suffer, as to do,
Our strength is equal, nor the law unjust
That so ordains; this was at first resolved,
If we were wise, against so great a foe
Contending, and so doubtful what might fall.
I laugh when those who at the spear are bold
And venturous, if that fail them, shrink, and fear
What yet they know must follow – to endure
Exile, or ignominy, or bonds, or pain,
The sentence of their conqueror: this is now
Our doom; which if we can sustain and bear,
Our supreme foe in time may much remit
His anger, and perhaps, thus far removed,
Not mind us not offending, satisfied
With what is punished; whence these raging fires
Will slacken, if his breath stir not their flames.
Our purer essence then will overcome
Their noxious vapour, or, inured, not feel,

Or, changed at length, and to the place conformed
In temper and in nature, will receive
Familiar the fierce heat; and, void of pain,
This horror will grow mild, this darkness light;
Besides what hope the never-ending flight
Of future days may bring, what chance, what change
Worth waiting – since our present lot appears
For happy though but ill, for ill not worst,
If we procure not to ourselves more woe.'

    Thus Belial, with words clothed in reason's garb,
Counselled ignoble ease and peaceful sloth,
Not peace; and after him thus Mammon spake:

    'Either to disenthrone the king of heaven
We war, if war be best, or to regain
Our own right lost; him to unthrone we then
May hope, when everlasting Fate shall yield
To fickle Chance, and Chaos judge the strife:
The former, vain to hope, argues as vain
The latter; for what place can be for us
Within heaven's bound, unless heaven's lord supreme
We overpower? Suppose he should relent,
And publish grace to all, on promise made
Of new subjection; with what eyes could we
Stand in his presence humble, and receive
Strict laws imposed, to celebrate his throne
With warbled hymns, and to his Godhead sing
Forced halleluiahs, while he lordly sits

Our envied sovereign, and his altar breathes
Ambrosial odours and ambrosial flowers,
Our servile offerings? This must be our task
In heaven, this our delight; how wearisome
Eternity so spent in worship paid
To whom we hate. Let us not then pursue,
By force impossible, by leave obtained
Unacceptable, though in heaven, our state
Of splendid vassalage; but rather seek
Our own good from ourselves, and from our own
Live to ourselves, though in this vast recess,
Free and to none accountable, preferring
Hard liberty before the easy yoke
Of servile pomp. Our greatness will appear
Then most conspicuous when great things of small,
Useful of hurtful, prosperous of adverse,
We can create, and in what place so e'er
Thrive under evil, and work ease out of pain
Through labour and endurance. This deep world
Of darkness do we dread? How oft amidst
Thick clouds and dark doth heaven's all-ruling sire
Choose to reside, his glory unobscured,
And with the majesty of darkness round
Covers his throne, from whence deep thunders roar,
Mustering their rage, and heaven resembles hell?
As he our darkness, cannot we his light
Imitate when we please? This desert soil

Wants not her hidden lustre, gems and gold;
Nor want we skill or art from whence to raise
Magnificence; and what can heaven show more?
Our torments also may, in length of time,
Become our elements, these piercing fires
As soft as now severe, our temper changed
Into their temper; which must needs remove
The sensible of pain. All things invite
To peaceful counsels, and the settled state
Of order, how in safety best we may
Compose our present evils, with regard
Of what we are and where, dismissing quite
All thoughts of war; ye have what I advise.'

    He scarce had finished, when such murmur filled
The assembly as when hollow rocks retain
The sound of blustering winds, which all night long
Had roused the sea, now with hoarse cadence lull
Seafaring men o'erwatched, whose bark by chance,
Or pinnace anchors in a craggy bay
After the tempest; such applause was heard
As Mammon ended, and his sentence pleased,
Advising peace: for such another field
They dreaded worse than hell; so much the fear
Of thunder and the sword of Michaël
Wrought still within them; and no less desire
To found this nether empire, which might rise,
By policy and long process of time,

In emulation opposite to heaven.
Which when Beëlzebub perceived – than whom,
Satan except, none higher sat – with grave
Aspect he rose, and in his rising seemed
A pillar of state; deep on his front engraven
Deliberation sat, and public care;
And princely counsel in his face yet shone,
Majestic, though in ruin; sage he stood,
With Atlantean shoulders, fit to bear
The weight of mightiest monarchies; his look
Drew audience and attention still as night
Or summer's noontide air, while thus he spake:
    'Thrones and imperial powers, offspring of heaven,
Ethereal virtues; or these titles now
Must we renounce, and, changing style, be called
Princes of hell? For so the popular vote
Inclines – here to continue, and build up here
A growing empire; doubtless; while we dream,
And know not that the king of heaven hath doomed
This place our dungeon – not our safe retreat
Beyond his potent arm, to live exempt
From heaven's high jurisdiction, in new league
Banded against his throne, but to remain
In strictest bondage, though thus far removed,
Under the inevitable curb, reserved
His captive multitude; for he, be sure,
In height or depth, still first and last will reign

Sole king, and of his kingdom lose no part
By our revolt, but over hell extend
His empire, and with iron sceptre rule
Us here, as with his golden those in heaven.
What sit we then projecting peace and war?
War hath determined us, and foiled with loss
Irreparable; terms of peace yet none
Vouchsafed or sought; for what peace will be given
To us enslaved, but custody severe,
And stripes and arbitrary punishment
Inflicted? And what peace can we return,
But, to our power, hostility and hate,
Untamed reluctance, and revenge, though slow,
Yet ever plotting how the conqueror least
May reap his conquest, and may least rejoice
In doing what we most in suffering feel?
Nor will occasion want, nor shall we need
With dangerous expedition to invade
Heaven, whose high walls fear no assault or siege,
Or ambush from the deep. What if we find
Some easier enterprise? There is a place
(If ancient and prophetic fame in heaven
Err not) – another world, the happy seat
Of some new race called Man, about this time
To be created like to us, though less
In power and excellence, but favoured more
Of him who rules above; so was his will

Pronounced among the gods, and by an oath
That shook heaven's whole circumference, confirmed.
Thither let us bend all our thoughts, to learn
What creatures there inhabit, of what mould
Or substance, how endued, and what their power
And where their weakness; how attempted best
By force or subtlety; though heaven be shut,
And heaven's high arbitrator sit secure
In his own strength, this place may lie exposed,
The utmost border of his kingdom, left
To their defence who hold it: here perhaps
Some advantageous acts may be achieved
By sudden onset – either with hell-fire
To waste his whole creation, or possess
All as our own, and drive, as we are driven,
The puny habitants; or if not drive,
Seduce them to our party, that their God
May prove their foe, and with repenting hand
Abolish his own works. This would surpass
Common revenge, and interrupt his joy
In our confusion, and our joy upraise
In his disturbance; when his darling sons,
Hurled headlong to partake with us, shall curse
Their frail original, and faded bliss –
Faded so soon. Advise if this be worth
Attempting, or to sit in darkness here
Hatching vain empires.' Thus Beëlzebub

Pleaded his devilish counsel – first devised
By Satan, and in part proposed: for whence,
But from the author of all ill, could spring
So deep a malice, to confound the race
Of mankind in one root, and earth with hell
To mingle and involve, done all to spite
The great creator? But their spite still serves
His glory to augment. The bold design
Pleased highly those infernal states, and joy
Sparkled in all their eyes; with full assent
They vote: whereat his speech he thus renews:

    'Well have ye judged, well ended long debate,
Synod of gods, and like to what ye are,
Great things resolved, which from the lowest deep
Will once more lift us up, in spite of fate,
Nearer our ancient seat – perhaps in view
Of those bright confines, whence, with neighbouring
      arms
And opportune excursion, we may chance
Re-enter heaven; or else in some mild zone
Dwell, not unvisited of heaven's fair light
Secure, and at the brightening orient beam
Purge off this gloom: the soft delicious air,
To heal the scar of these corrosive fires,
Shall breathe her balm. But, first, whom shall we send
In search of this new world, whom shall we find
Sufficient? Who shall tempt with wandering feet

The dark, unbottomed, infinite abyss,
And through the palpable obscure find out
His uncouth way, or spread his airy flight,
Upborne with indefatigable wings
Over the vast abrupt, ere he arrive
The happy isle? What strength, what art, can then
Suffice, or what evasion bear him safe,
Through the strict senteries and stations thick
Of angels watching round? Here he had need
All circumspection, and we now no less
Choice in our suffrage; for on whom we send
The weight of all, and our last hope, relies.'

  This said, he sat; and expectation held
His look suspense, awaiting who appeared
To second, or oppose, or undertake
The perilous attempt; but all sat mute,
Pondering the danger with deep thoughts; and each
In other's countenance read his own dismay,
Astonished; none among the choice and prime
Of those heaven-warring champions could be found
So hardy as to proffer or accept,
Alone, the dreadful voyage; till at last
Satan, whom now transcendent glory raised
Above his fellows, with monarchal pride
Conscious of highest worth, unmoved thus spake:

  'O progeny of heaven, empyreal thrones;
With reason hath deep silence and demur

Seized us, though undismayed; long is the way
And hard, that out of hell leads up to light;
Our prison strong, this huge convex of fire,
Outrageous to devour, immures us round
Ninefold; and gates of burning adamant,
Barred over us, prohibit all egress.
These passed, if any pass, the void profound
Of unessential night receives him next,
Wide gaping, and with utter loss of being
Threatens him, plunged in that abortive gulf.
If thence he scape, into whatever world,
Or unknown region, what remains him less
Than unknown dangers, and as hard escape?
But I should ill become this throne, O peers,
And this imperial sovereignty, adorned
With splendour, armed with power, if aught proposed
And judged of public moment in the shape
Of difficulty or danger, could deter
Me from attempting. Wherefore do I assume
These royalties, and not refuse to reign,
Refusing to accept as great a share
Of hazard as of honour, due alike
To him who reigns, and so much to him due
Of hazard more as he above the rest
High honoured sits? Go therefore mighty powers,
Terror of heaven, though fallen; intend at home,
While here shall be our home, what best may ease

The present misery, and render hell
More tolerable; if there be cure or charm
To respite or deceive, or slack the pain
Of this ill mansion: intermit no watch
Against a wakeful foe, while I abroad
Through all the coasts of dark destruction seek
Deliverance for us all; this enterprise
None shall partake with me.' Thus saying, rose
The monarch, and prevented all reply;
Prudent lest, from his resolution raised,
Others among the chief might offer now
(Certain to be refused) what erst they feared,
And so refused might in opinion stand
His rivals, winning cheap the high repute
Which he through hazard huge must earn. But they
Dreaded not more the adventure than his voice
Forbidding; and at once with him they rose;
Their rising all at once was as the sound
Of thunder heard remote. Towards him they bend
With awful reverence prone, and as a god
Extol him equal to the highest in heaven.
Nor failed they to express how much they praised
That for the general safety he despised
His own: for neither do the spirits damned
Lose all their virtue; lest bad men should boast
Their specious deeds on earth, which glory excites,
Or close ambition varnished o'er with zeal.

(Lines 1–485)

    Meanwhile the adversary of God and man,
Satan, with thoughts inflamed of highest design,
Puts on swift wings, and toward the gates of hell
Explores his solitary flight; sometimes
He scours the right hand coast, sometimes the left;
Now shaves with level wing the deep, then soars
Up to the fiery concave towering high.
As when far off at sea a fleet descried
Hangs in the clouds, by equinoctial winds
Close sailing from Bengala, or the isles
Of Ternate and Tidore, whence merchants bring
Their spicy drugs; they on the trading flood,
Through the wide Ethiopian to the Cape,
Ply stemming nightly toward the pole: so seemed
Far off the flying fiend; at last appear
Hell-bounds, high reaching to the horrid roof,
And thrice threefold the gates; three folds were brass,
Three iron, three of adamantine rock,
Impenetrable, impaled with circling fire,
Yet unconsumed. Before the gates there sat
On either side a formidable shape;
The one seemed woman to the waist, and fair,
But ended foul in many a scaly fold,
Voluminous and vast – a serpent armed
With mortal sting; about her middle round
A cry of hell hounds never ceasing barked
With wide Cerberean mouths full loud, and rung

A hideous peal; yet, when they list, would creep,
If aught disturbed their noise, into her womb,
And kennel there; yet there still barked and howled
Within unseen. Far less abhorred than these
Vexed Scylla, bathing in the sea that parts
Calabria from the hoarse Trinacrian shore;
Nor uglier follow the night-hag, when, called
In secret, riding through the air she comes,
Lured with the smell of infant blood, to dance
With Lapland witches, while the labouring moon
Eclipses at their charms. The other shape –
If shape it might be called that shape had none
Distinguishable in member, joint, or limb;
Or substance might be called that shadow seemed,
For each seemed either – black it stood as night,
Fierce as ten Furies, terrible as hell,
And shook a dreadful dart: what seemed his head
The likeness of a kingly crown had on.
Satan was now at hand, and from his seat
The monster moving onward came as fast
With horrid strides; hell trembled as he strode.
The undaunted fiend what this might be admired,
Admired, not feared – God and his Son except,
Created thing nought valued he nor shunned –
And with disdainful look thus first began:
    'Whence and what art thou, execrable shape,
That dar'st, though grim and terrible, advance

Thy miscreated front athwart my way
To yonder gates? Through them I mean to pass,
That be assured, without leave asked of thee:
Retire, or taste thy folly, and learn by proof,
Hell-born, not to contend with spirits of heaven.'
    To whom the goblin, full of wrath, replied:
'Art thou that traitor angel, art thou he,
Who first broke peace in heaven and faith, till then
Unbroken, and in proud rebellious arms
Drew after him the third part of heaven's sons,
Conjured against the highest – for which both thou
And they outcast from God, are here condemned
To waste eternal days in woe and pain?
And reckon'st thou thyself with spirits of heaven,
Hell-doomed, and breath'st defiance here and scorn,
Where I reign king, and to enrage thee more,
Thy king and lord? Back to thy punishment,
False fugitive, and to thy speed add wings,
Lest with a whip of scorpions I pursue
Thy lingering, or with one stroke of this dart
Strange horror seize thee, and pangs unfelt before.'
    So spake the grisly terror, and in shape,
So speaking and so threatening, grew tenfold
More dreadful and deform; on the other side,
Incensed with indignation, Satan stood
Unterrified, and like a comet burned,
That fires the length of Ophiucus huge

In the arctic sky, and from his horrid hair
Shakes pestilence and war. Each at the head
Levelled his deadly aim; their fatal hands
No second stroke intend; and such a frown
Each cast at the other as when two black clouds,
With heaven's artillery fraught, come rattling on
Over the Caspian – then stand front to front
Hovering a space, till winds the signal blow
To join their dark encounter in mid air;
So frowned the mighty combatants that hell
Grew darker at their frown; so matched they stood;
For never but once more was either like
To meet so great a foe; and now great deeds
Had been achieved, whereof all hell had rung,
Had not the snaky sorceress, that sat
Fast by hell gate and kept the fatal key,
Risen, and with hideous outcry rushed between.

   'O father, what intends thy hand,' she cried,
'Against thy only son? What fury, O son,
Possesses thee to bend that mortal dart
Against thy father's head? And know'st for whom?
For him who sits above, and laughs the while
At thee, ordained his drudge to execute
Whate'er his wrath, which he calls justice, bids –
His wrath, which one day will destroy ye both.'

   She spake, and at her words the hellish pest
Forbore; then these to her Satan returned;

'So strange thy outcry, and thy words so strange
Thou interposest, that my sudden hand,
Prevented, spares to tell thee yet by deeds
What it intends, till first I know of thee
What thing thou art, thus double-formed, and why,
In this infernal vale first me, thou call'st
Me father, and that phantasm call'st my son.
I know thee not, nor ever saw till now
Sight more detestable than him and thee.'
　　To whom thus the portress of hell gate replied:
'Hast thou forgot me, then; and do I seem
Now in thine eye so foul? – once deemed so fair
In heaven, when at the assembly, and in sight
Of all the seraphim with thee combined
In bold conspiracy against heaven's king,
All on a sudden miserable pain
Surprised thee, dim thine eyes and dizzy swum
In darkness, while thy head flames thick and fast
Threw forth, till on the left side opening wide,
Likest to thee in shape and countenance bright,
Then shining heavenly fair, a goddess armed,
Out of thy head I sprung; amazement seized
All the host of heaven; back they recoiled afraid
At first, and called me Sin, and for a sign
Portentous held me; but, familiar grown,
I pleased, and with attractive graces won
The most averse – thee chiefly, who, full oft

Thyself in me thy perfect image viewing,
Becam'st enamoured; and such joy thou took'st
With me in secret that my womb conceived
A growing burden. Meanwhile war arose,
And fields were fought in heaven: wherein remained
(For what could else?) to our almighty foe
Clear victory; to our part loss and rout
Through all the empyrean; down they fell,
Driven headlong from the pitch of heaven, down
Into this deep, and in the general fall
I also: at which time this powerful key
Into my hand was given, with charge to keep
These gates for ever shut, which none can pass
Without my opening. Pensive here I sat
Alone; but long I sat not, till my womb,
Pregnant by thee, and now excessive grown,
Prodigious motion felt and rueful throes.
At last this odious offspring whom thou seest,
Thine own begotten, breaking violent way,
Tore through my entrails, that with fear and pain
Distorted, all my nether shape thus grew
Transformed: but he my inbred enemy
Forth issued, brandishing his fatal dart,
Made to destroy: I fled, and cried out "Death";
Hell trembled at the hideous name, and sighed
From all her caves, and back resounded "Death".
I fled, but he pursued (though more, it seems,

Inflamed with lust than rage) and swifter far,
Me overtook, his mother, all dismayed,
And, in embraces forcible and foul
Engendering with me, of that rape begot
These yelling monsters, that with ceaseless cry
Surround me, as thou saw'st – hourly conceived
And hourly born, with sorrow infinite
To me; for, when they list, into the womb
That bred them they return, and howl, and gnaw
My bowels, their repast; then, bursting forth
Afresh, with conscious terrors vex me round,
That rest or intermission none I find.
Before mine eyes in opposition sits
Grim Death, my son and foe, who sets them on,
And me, his parent, would full soon devour
For want of other prey, but that he knows
His end with mine involved, and knows that I
Should prove a bitter morsel, and his bane,
Whenever that shall be: so Fate pronounced.
But thou, O father, I forewarn thee, shun
His deadly arrow; neither vainly hope
To be invulnerable in those bright arms,
Though tempered heavenly; for that mortal dint,
Save he who reigns above, none can resist.'
    She finished, and the subtle fiend his lore
Soon learned, now milder, and thus answered smooth:
'Dear daughter – since thou claim'st me for thy sire,

And my fair son here show'st me, the dear pledge
Of dalliance had with thee in heaven, and joys
Then sweet, now sad to mention, through dire change
Befallen us unforeseen, unthought-of – know
I come no enemy, but to set free
From out this dark and dismal house of pain
Both him and thee, and all the heavenly host
Of spirits that, in our just pretences armed,
Fell with us from on high; from them I go
This uncouth errand sole, and one for all
Myself expose, with lonely steps to tread
The unfounded deep, and through the void immense
To search, with wandering quest, a place foretold
Should be – and, by concurring signs, ere now
Created vast and round – a place of bliss
In the purlieus of heaven; and therein placed
A race of upstart creatures, to supply
Perhaps our vacant room, though more removed,
Lest heaven, surcharged with potent multitude,
Might hap to move new broils; be this, or aught
Than this more secret, now designed, I haste
To know; and this once known, shall soon return,
And bring yet to the place where thou and Death
Shall dwell at ease, and up and down unseen
Wing silently the buxom air, embalmed
With odours; there ye shall be fed and filled
Immeasurably: all things shall be your prey.'

He ceased, for both seemed highly pleased, and Death
Grinned horrible a ghastly smile, to hear
His famine should be filled, and blessed his maw
Destined to that good hour; no less rejoiced
His mother bad, and thus bespake her sire:
　'The key of this infernal pit, by due
And by command of heaven's all-powerful king,
I keep, by him forbidden to unlock
These adamantine gates; against all force
Death ready stands to interpose his dart,
Fearless to be o'ermatched by living might.
But what owe I to his commands above,
Who hates me, and hath hither thrust me down
Into this gloom of Tartarus profound,
To sit in hateful office here confined,
Inhabitant of heaven and heavenly born –
Here in perpetual agony and pain,
With terrors and with clamours compassed round
Of mine own brood, that on my bowels feed?
Thou art my father, thou my author, thou
My being gav'st me; whom should I obey
But thee, whom follow? Thou wilt bring me soon
To that new world of light and bliss, among
The gods who live at ease, where I shall reign
At thy right hand voluptuous, as beseems
Thy daughter and thy darling, without end.'
　Thus saying, from her side the fatal key,

Sad instrument of all our woe, she took;
And, towards the gate rolling her bestial train,
Forthwith the huge portcullis high updrew,
Which, but herself, not all the Stygian powers
Could once have moved; then in the key-hole turns
The intricate wards, and every bolt and bar
Of massy iron or solid rock with ease
Unfastens; on a sudden open fly,
With impetuous recoil and jarring sound,
The infernal doors, and on their hinges grate
Harsh thunder, that the lowest bottom shook
Of Erebus. She opened, but to shut
Excelled her power: the gates wide open stood,
That with extended wings a bannered host,
Under spread ensigns marching, might pass through
With horse and chariots ranked in loose array;
So wide they stood, and like a furnace-mouth
Cast forth redounding smoke and ruddy flame.
Before their eyes in sudden view appear
The secrets of the hoary deep – a dark
Illimitable ocean without bound,
Without dimension; where length, breadth, and height,
And time and place, are lost; where eldest Night
And Chaos, ancestors of Nature, hold
Eternal anarchy, amidst the noise
Of endless wars, and by confusion stand.
For Hot, Cold, Moist, and Dry, four champions fierce,

Strive here for mastery, and to battle bring
Their embryon atoms: they around the flag
Of each his faction, in their several clans,
Light-armed or heavy, sharp, smooth, swift, or slow,
Swarm populous, unnumbered as the sands
Of Barca or Cyrene's torrid soil,
Levied to side with warring winds, and poise
Their lighter wings. To whom these most adhere
He rules a moment: Chaos umpire sits,
And by decision more embroils the fray
By which he reigns: next him, high arbiter,
Chance governs all. Into this wild abyss,
The womb of Nature, and perhaps her grave,
Of neither sea, nor shore, nor air, nor fire,
But all these in their pregnant causes mixed
Confusedly, and which thus must ever fight,
Unless the almighty maker them ordain
His dark materials to create more worlds –
Into this wild abyss the wary fiend
Stood on the brink of hell and looked a while,
Pondering his voyage; for no narrow frith
He had to cross. Nor was his ear less pealed
With noises loud and ruinous (to compare
Great things with small) than when Bellona storms
With all her battering engines, bent to raze
Some capital city; or less than if this frame
Of heaven were falling, and these elements

In mutiny had from her axle torn
The steadfast earth. At last his sail-broad vans
He spreads for flight, and, in the surging smoke
Uplifted, spurns the ground; thence many a league,
As in a cloudy chair, ascending rides
Audacious, but that seat soon failing, meets
A vast vacuity; all unawares,
Fluttering his pennons vain, plumb-down he drops
Ten thousand fathom deep, and to this hour
Down had been falling, had not by ill chance
The strong rebuff of some tumultuous cloud,
Instinct with fire and nitre, hurried him
As many miles aloft; that fury stayed –
Quenched in a boggy Syrtis, neither sea,
Nor good dry land – nigh foundered, on he fares,
Treading the crude consistence, half on foot,
Half flying; behoves him now both oar and sail.
As when a griffin through the wilderness
With wingèd course, o'er hill or moory dale,
Pursues the Arimaspian, who by stealth
Had from his wakeful custody purloined
The guarded gold; so eagerly the fiend
O'er bog or steep, through strait, rough, dense, or rare,
With head, hands, wings or feet, pursues his way,
And swims, or sinks, or wades, or creeps, or flies;
At length a universal hubbub wild
Of stunning sounds, and voices all confused,

Borne through the hollow dark, assaults his ear
With loudest vehemence; thither he plies
Undaunted, to meet there whatever power
Or spirit of the nethermost abyss
Might in that noise reside, of whom to ask
Which way the nearest coast of darkness lies
Bordering on light; when straight behold the throne
Of Chaos, and his dark pavilion spread
Wide on the wasteful deep; with him enthroned
Sat sable-vested Night, eldest of things,
The consort of his reign; and by them stood
Orcus and Ades, and the dreaded name
Of Demogorgon; Rumour next, and Chance,
And Tumult and Confusion, all embroiled,
And Discord with a thousand various mouths.
    To whom Satan, turning boldly, thus: 'Ye powers
And spirits of this nethermost abyss,
Chaos and ancient Night, I come no spy
With purpose to explore or to disturb
The secrets of your realm, but by constraint
Wandering this darksome desert, as my way
Lies through your spacious empire up to light
Alone and without guide, half lost, I seek
What readiest path leads where your gloomy bounds
Confine with heaven; or if some other place,
From your dominion won, the ethereal king
Possesses lately, thither to arrive

I travel this profound; direct my course:
Directed, no mean recompense it brings
To your behoof, if I that region lost,
All usurpation thence expelled, reduce
To her original darkness and your sway
(Which is my present journey) and once more
Erect the standard there of ancient Night.
Yours be the advantage all, mine the revenge.'
    Thus Satan; and him thus the anarch old,
With faltering speech and visage incomposed,
Answered: 'I know thee, stranger, who thou art –
That mighty leading angel, who of late
Made head against heaven's king, though overthrown.
I saw and heard; for such a numerous host
Fled not in silence through the frighted deep,
With ruin upon ruin, rout on rout,
Confusion worse confounded; and heaven gates
Poured out by millions her victorious bands,
Pursuing. I upon my frontiers here
Keep residence; if all I can will serve
That little which is left so to defend,
Encroached on still through our intestine broils
Weakening the sceptre of old Night: first hell,
Your dungeon, stretching far and wide beneath;
Now lately heaven and earth, another world
Hung o'er my realm, linked in a golden chain
To that side heaven from whence your legions fell;

If that way be your walk, you have not far;
So much the nearer danger; go, and speed;
Havoc and spoil and ruin are my gain.'
    He ceased; and Satan stayed not to reply,
But glad that now his sea should find a shore,
With fresh alacrity and force renewed
Springs upward, like a pyramid of fire,
Into the wild expanse, and through the shock
Of fighting elements, on all sides round
Environed, wins his way; harder beset
And more endangered than when Argo passed
Through Bosporus betwixt the jostling rocks,
Or when Ulysses on the larboard shunned
Charybdis, and by the other whirlpool steered.
So he with difficulty and labour hard
Moved on, with difficulty and labour he;
But, he once passed, soon after, when man fell,
Strange alteration! Sin and Death amain,
Following his track – such was the will of heaven –
Paved after him a broad and beaten way
Over the dark abyss, whose boiling gulf
Tamely endured a bridge of wondrous length,
From hell continued, reaching the utmost orb
Of this frail world; by which the spirits perverse
With easy intercourse pass to and fro
To tempt or punish mortals, except whom
God and good angels guard by special grace.

But now at last the sacred influence
Of light appears, and from the walls of heaven
Shoots far into the bosom of dim Night
A glimmering dawn; here Nature first begins
Her farthest verge, and Chaos to retire,
As from her outmost works, a broken foe,
With tumult less and with less hostile din;
That Satan with less toil, and now with ease,
Wafts on the calmer wave by dubious light,
And, like a weather-beaten vessel, holds
Gladly the port, though shrouds and tackle torn;
Or in the emptier waste, resembling air,
Weighs his spread wings, at leisure to behold
Far off the empyreal heaven, extended wide
In circuit, undetermined square or round,
With opal towers and battlements adorned
Of living sapphire, once his native seat;
And, fast by, hanging in a golden chain,
This pendent world, in bigness as a star
Of smallest magnitude close by the moon.
Thither, full fraught with mischievous revenge,
Accursed, and in a cursed hour, he hies.

(Lines 629–1055)

BOOK III

THE ARGUMENT

God, sitting on his throne, sees Satan flying towards
this world, then newly created; shows him to the Son,
who sat at his right hand; foretells the success of Satan
in perverting mankind; clears his own justice and
wisdom from all imputation, having created man free,
and able enough to have withstood his tempter; yet
declares his purpose of grace towards him, in regard
he fell not of his own malice, as did Satan, but by him
seduced. The Son of God renders praises to his Father
for the manifestation of his gracious purpose towards
man: but God again declares that grace cannot be
extended towards man without the satisfaction of
divine justice; man hath offended the majesty of God
by aspiring to Godhead, and therefore, with all his
progeny, devoted to death, must die, unless some one
can be found sufficient to answer for his offence, and
undergo his punishment. The Son of God freely offers
himself a ransom for man: the Father accepts him,
ordains his incarnation, pronounces his exaltation
above all names in heaven and earth; commands all
the angels to adore him; they obey, and hymning to
their harps in full choir, celebrate the Father and the
Son. Meanwhile Satan alights upon the bare convex
of this world's outermost orb; where wandering he

first finds a place since called the Limbo of Vanity; what persons and things fly up thither: thence comes to the gate of heaven, described ascending by stairs, and the waters above the firmament that flow about it; his passage thence to the orb of the sun: he finds there Uriel, the regent of that orb, but first changes himself into the shape of a meaner angel, and pretending a zealous desire to behold the new creation, and man whom God had placed here, enquires of him the place of his habitation, and is directed: alights first on Mount Niphates.

*

Now had the almighty Father from above,
From the pure empyrean where he sits
High throned above all height, bent down his eye,
His own works and their works at once to view:
About him all the sanctities of heaven
Stood thick as stars, and from his sight received
Beatitude past utterance; on his right
The radiant image of his glory sat,
His only Son; on earth he first beheld
Our two first parents, yet the only two
Of mankind, in the happy garden placed,
Reaping immortal fruits of joy and love,
Uninterrupted joy, unrivalled love,
In blissful solitude; he then surveyed

Hell and the gulf between, and Satan there
Coasting the wall of heaven on this side night,
In the dun air sublime, and ready now
To stoop with wearied wings, and willing feet,
On the bare outside of this world, that seemed
Firm land imbosomed without firmament,
Uncertain which, in ocean or in air.
Him God beholding from his prospect high,
Wherein past, present, future, he beholds,
Thus to his only Son foreseeing spake:
    'Only-begotten Son, seest thou what rage
Transports our adversary, whom no bounds
Prescribed, no bars of hell, nor all the chains
Heaped on him there, nor yet the main abyss
Wide interrupt, can hold; so bent he seems
On desperate revenge, that shall redound
Upon his own rebellious head. And now
Through all restraint broke loose he wings his way
Not far off heaven, in the precincts of light,
Directly towards the new-created world,
And man there placed, with purpose to assay
If him by force he can destroy, or, worse,
By some false guile pervert: and shall pervert;
For man will hearken to his glozing lies,
And easily transgress the sole command,
Sole pledge of his obedience: so will fall
He and his faithless progeny: whose fault?

Whose but his own? Ingrate, he had of me
All he could have; I made him just and right,
Sufficient to have stood, though free to fall.
Such I created all the ethereal powers
And spirits, both them who stood and them who failed:
Freely they stood who stood, and fell who fell.
Not free, what proof could they have given sincere
Of true allegiance, constant faith, or love,
Where only what they needs must do appeared,
Not what they would? What praise could they receive,
What pleasure I, from such obedience paid,
When will and reason (reason also is choice),
Useless and vain, of freedom both despoiled,
Made passive both, had served necessity,
Not me? They therefore as to right belonged
So were created, nor can justly accuse
Their maker, or their making, or their fate,
As if predestination overruled
Their will, disposed by absolute decree
Or high foreknowledge; they themselves decreed
Their own revolt, not I: if I foreknew,
Foreknowledge had no influence on their fault,
Which had no less proved certain unforeknown.
So without least impulse or shadow of fate,
Or aught by me immutably foreseen,
They trespass, authors to themselves in all,
Both what they judge and what they choose; for so

I formed them free, and free they must remain
Till they enthral themselves: I else must change
Their nature, and revoke the high decree
Unchangeable, eternal, which ordained
Their freedom; they themselves ordained their fall.
The first sort by their own suggestion fell,
Self-tempted, self-depraved: man falls, deceived
By the other first: man, therefore, shall find grace,
The other, none; in mercy and justice both,
Through heaven and earth, so shall my glory excel;
But mercy, first and last, shall brightest shine.'
   Thus while God spake ambrosial fragrance filled
All heaven, and in the blessed spirits elect
Sense of new joy ineffable diffused:
Beyond compare the Son of God was seen
Most glorious; in him all his Father shone
Substantially expressed, and in his face
Divine compassion visibly appeared,
Love without end, and without measure grace;
Which uttering, thus he to his Father spake:
   'O Father, gracious was that word which closed
Thy sovereign sentence, that man should find grace;
For which both heaven and earth shall high extol
Thy praises, with the innumerable sound
Of hymns and sacred songs, wherewith thy throne
Encompassed shall resound thee ever blessed.
For, should man finally be lost – should man,

Thy creature late so loved, thy youngest son,
Fall circumvented thus by fraud, though joined
With his own folly? That be from thee far,
That far be from thee, Father, who art judge
Of all things made, and judgest only right.
Or shall the adversary thus obtain
His end, and frustrate thine? Shall he fulfil
His malice, and thy goodness bring to naught
Or proud return, though to his heavier doom
Yet with revenge accomplished, and to hell
Draw after him the whole race of mankind,
By him corrupted? Or wilt thou thyself
Abolish thy creation, and unmake,
For him, what for thy glory thou hast made?
So should thy goodness and thy greatness both
Be questioned and blasphemed without defence.'
    To whom the great creator thus replied:
'O Son, in whom my soul hath chief delight,
Son of my bosom, Son who art alone
My word, my wisdom, and effectual might,
All hast thou spoken as my thoughts are, all
As my eternal purpose hath decreed:
Man shall not quite be lost, but saved who will,
Yet not of will in him, but grace in me
Freely vouchsafed; once more I will renew
His lapsèd powers, though forfeit, and enthralled
By sin to foul exorbitant desires:

Upheld by me, yet once more he shall stand
On even ground against his mortal foe –
By me upheld, that he may know how frail
His fallen condition is, and to me owe
All his deliverance, and to none but me.
Some I have chosen of peculiar grace,
Elect above the rest; so is my will:
The rest shall hear me call, and oft be warned
Their sinful state, and to appease betimes
The incensèd Deity, while offered grace
Invites; for I will clear their senses dark
What may suffice, and soften stony hearts
To pray, repent, and bring obedience due.
To prayer, repentance, and obedience due,
Though but endeavoured with sincere intent,
Mine ear shall not be slow, mine eye not shut.
And I will place within them as a guide
My umpire conscience; whom if they will hear,
Light after light well used they shall attain,
And to the end persisting safe arrive.
This my long sufferance, and my day of grace,
They who neglect and scorn shall never taste;
But hard be hardened, blind be blinded more,
That they may stumble on, and deeper fall;
And none but such from mercy I exclude.
But yet all is not done; man disobeying,
Disloyal, breaks his fealty, and sins

Against the high supremacy of heaven,
Affecting Godhead, and so losing all,
To expiate his treason hath naught left,
But to destruction sacred and devote,
He with his whole posterity must die –
Die he or justice must; unless for him
Some other, able, and as willing, pay
The rigid satisfaction, death for death.
Say heavenly powers, where shall we find such love?
Which of ye will be mortal, to redeem
Man's mortal crime, and just, the unjust to save?
Dwells in all heaven charity so dear?'

    He asked, but all the heavenly choir stood mute,
And silence was in heaven: on man's behalf
Patron or intercessor none appeared –
Much less that durst upon his own head draw
The deadly forfeiture, and ransom set.
And now without redemption all mankind
Must have been lost, adjudged to death and hell
By doom severe, had not the Son of God,
In whom the fullness dwells of love divine,
His dearest mediation thus renewed:

    'Father, thy word is passed, man shall find grace;
And shall Grace not find means, that finds her way,
The speediest of thy wingèd messengers,
To visit all thy creatures, and to all
Comes unprevented, unimplored, unsought?

Happy for man, so coming; he her aid
Can never seek, once dead in sins and lost –
Atonement for himself, or offering meet,
Indebted and undone, hath none to bring;
Behold me, then: me for him, life for life,
I offer; on me let thine anger fall;
Account me man: I for his sake will leave
Thy bosom, and this glory next to thee
Freely put off, and for him lastly die
Well pleased; on me let Death wreak all his rage;
Under his gloomy power I shall not long
Lie vanquished; thou hast given me to possess
Life in myself for ever; by thee I live;
Though now to Death I yield, and am his due,
All that of me can die, yet that debt paid,
Thou wilt not leave me in the loathsome grave
His prey, nor suffer my unspotted soul
For ever with corruption there to dwell;
But I shall rise victorious, and subdue
My vanquisher, spoiled of his vaunted spoil;
Death his death's wound shall then receive, and stoop
Inglorious, of his mortal sting disarmed.
I through the ample air in triumph high
Shall lead hell captive maugre hell, and show
The powers of darkness bound. Thou, at the sight
Pleased, out of heaven shall look down and smile,
While, by thee raised, I ruin all my foes –

Death last, and with his carcass glut the grave;
Then, with the multitude of my redeemed,
Shall enter heaven, long absent, and return,
Father, to see thy face, wherein no cloud
Of anger shall remain, but peace assured
And reconcilement; wrath shall be no more
Thenceforth, but in thy presence joy entire.'

His words here ended; but his meek aspect
Silent yet spake, and breathed immortal love
To mortal men, above which only shone
Filial obedience: as a sacrifice
Glad to be offered, he attends the will
Of his great Father. Admiration seized
All heaven, what this might mean, and whither tend,
Wondering; but soon the almighty thus replied:

'O thou in heaven and earth the only peace
Found out for mankind under wrath, O thou
My sole complacence! Well thou know'st how dear
To me are all my works; nor man the least,
Though last created, that for him I spare
Thee from my bosom and right hand, to save,
By losing thee a while, the whole race lost.
Thou, therefore, whom thou only canst redeem,
Their nature also to thy nature join;
And thyself man among men on earth,
Made flesh, when time shall be, of virgin seed,
By wondrous birth; be thou in Adam's room

The head of all mankind, though Adam's son.
As in him perish all men, so in thee,
As from a second root, shall be restored
As many as are restored; without thee, none.
His crime makes guilty all his sons; thy merit
Imputed, shall absolve them who renounce
Their own both righteous and unrighteous deeds,
And live in thee transplanted, and from thee
Receive new life. So man, as is most just,
Shall satisfy for man, be judged and die,
And dying rise, and rising with him raise
His brethren, ransomed with his own dear life.
So heavenly love shall outdo hellish hate,
Giving to death, and dying to redeem,
So dearly to redeem what hellish hate
So easily destroyed, and still destroys
In those who, when they may, accept not grace.
Nor shalt thou, by descending to assume
Man's nature, lessen or degrade thine own.
Because thou hast, though throned in highest bliss
Equal to God, and equally enjoying
God-life fruition, quitted all to save
A world from utter loss, and hast been found
By merit more than birthright Son of God –
Found worthiest to be so by being good,
Far more than great or high; because in thee
Love hath abounded more than glory abounds;

Therefore thy humiliation shall exalt
With thee thy manhood also to this throne:
Here shalt thou sit incarnate, here shalt reign
Both God and man, Son both of God and man,
Anointed universal king; all power
I give thee; reign for ever, and assume
Thy merits; under thee, as head supreme,
Thrones, princedoms, powers, dominions, I reduce:
All knees to thee shall bow of them that bide
In heaven, or earth, or under earth in hell;
When thou, attended gloriously from heaven,
Shalt in the sky appear, and from thee send
The summoning archangels to proclaim
Thy dread tribunal, forthwith from all winds
The living, and forthwith the cited dead
Of all past ages, to the general doom
Shall hasten; such a peal shall rouse their sleep.
Then all thy saints assembled, thou shalt judge
Bad men and angels; thy arraigned shall sink
Beneath thy sentence; hell, her numbers full,
Thenceforth shall be for ever shut. Meanwhile
The world shall burn, and from her ashes spring
New heaven and earth, wherein the just shall dwell,
And after all their tribulations long,
See golden days, fruitful of golden deeds,
With joy and love triumphing, and fair truth.
Then thou thy regal sceptre shalt lay by,

For regal sceptre then no more shall need;
God shall be all in all. But all ye gods,
Adore him who, to compass all this, dies;
Adore the Son, and honour him as me.'

(Lines 56–343)

*

Meanwhile, upon the firm opacous globe
Of this round world, whose first convex divides
The luminous inferior orbs, enclosed
From Chaos and the inroad of darkness old,
Satan alighted walks; a globe far off
It seemed, now seems a boundless continent,
Dark, waste, and wild, under the frown of Night
Starless exposed, and ever-threatening storms
Of Chaos blustering round, inclement sky,
Save on that side which from the wall of heaven,
Though distant far, some small reflection gains
Of glimmering air less vexed with tempest loud;
Here walked the fiend at large in spacious field.
As when a vulture, on Imaus bred,
Whose snowy ridge the roving Tartar bounds,
Dislodging from a region scarce of prey,
To gorge the flesh of lambs or yeanling kids
On hills where flocks are fed, flies toward the springs
Of Ganges or Hydaspes, Indian streams,

But in his way lights on the barren plains
Of Sericana, where Chineses drive
With sails and wind their cany wagons light;
So, on this windy sea of land, the fiend
Walked up and down alone, bent on his prey:
Alone, for other creature in this place,
Living or lifeless, to be found was none,
None yet, but store hereafter from the earth
Up hither like aerial vapours flew
Of all things transitory and vain, when sin
With vanity had filled the works of men –
Both all things vain, and all who in vain things
Built their fond hopes of glory or lasting fame,
Or happiness in this or the other life.
All who have their reward on earth, the fruits
Of painful superstition and blind zeal,
Naught seeking but the praise of men, here find
Fit retribution, empty as their deeds;
All the unaccomplished works of nature's hand,
Abortive, monstrous, or unkindly mixed,
Dissolved on earth, fleet hither, and in vain,
Till final dissolution, wander here –
Not in the neighbouring moon, as some have dreamed;
Those argent fields more likely habitants,
Translated saints, or middle spirits hold,
Betwixt the angelical and human kind;
Hither of ill-joined sons and daughters born

First from the ancient world those Giants came,
With many a vain exploit, though then renowned;
The builders next of Babel on the plain
Of Sennaär, and still with vain design
New Babels, had they wherewithal, would build:
Others came single; he who to be deemed
A god, leaped fondly into Aetna flames,
Empedocles; and he who to enjoy
Plato's Elysium, leaped into the sea,
Cleombrotus; and many more, too long,
Embryos and idiots, eremites and friars,
White, black and grey, with all their trumpery.
Here pilgrims roam, that strayed so far to seek
In Golgotha him dead who lives in heaven;
And they who, to be sure of Paradise,
Dying put on the weeds of Dominic,
Or in Franciscan think to pass disguised.
They pass the planets seven, and pass the fixed,
And that crystalline sphere whose balance weighs
The trepidation talked, and that first moved;
And now Saint Peter at heaven's wicket seems
To wait them with his keys, and now at foot
Of heaven's ascent they lift their feet, when lo
A violent cross wind from either coast
Blows them transverse ten thousand leagues awry,
Into the devious air; then might ye see
Cowls, hoods and habits, with their wearers, tossed

And fluttered into rags; then relics, beads,
Indulgences, dispenses, pardons, bulls,
The sport of winds: all these, upwhirled aloft,
Fly o'er the backside of the world far off
Into a limbo large and broad, since called
The Paradise of Fools, to few unknown
Long after, now unpeopled and untrod;
All this dark globe the fiend found as he passed,
And long he wandered, till at last a gleam
Of dawning light turned thitherward in haste
His travelled steps; far distant he descries,
Ascending by degrees magnificent
Up to the wall of heaven, a structure high;
At top whereof, but far more rich, appeared
The work as of a kingly palace gate,
With frontispiece of diamond and gold
Embellished; thick with sparkling orient gems
The portal shone, inimitable on earth
By model, or by shading pencil drawn.

(Lines 418–509)

BOOK IV

THE ARGUMENT

Satan, now in prospect of Eden, and nigh the place where he must now attempt the bold enterprise which he undertook alone against God and man, falls into many doubts with himself and many passions – fear, envy, and despair; but at length confirms himself in evil; journeys on to Paradise, whose outward prospect and situation is described; overleaps the bounds; sits, in the shape of a cormorant, on the tree of life, as highest in the garden, to look about him. The garden described; Satan's first sight of Adam and Eve; his wonder at their excellent form and happy state, but with resolution to work their fall; overhears their discourse; thence gathers that the tree of knowledge was forbidden them to eat of under penalty of death, and thereon intends to found his temptation by seducing them to transgress; then leaves them a while, to know further of their state by some other means. Meanwhile Uriel, descending on a sunbeam, warns Gabriel, who had in charge the gate of Paradise, that some evil spirit had escaped the deep, and passed at noon by his sphere, in the shape of a good angel, down to Paradise, discovered after by his furious gestures in the mount. Gabriel promises to find him ere morning. Night coming on, Adam and Eve discourse of going

to their rest: their bower described; their evening
worship. Gabriel, drawing forth his bands of night-
watch to walk the round of Paradise, appoints two
strong angels to Adam's bower, lest the evil spirit
should be there doing some harm to Adam or Eve
sleeping: there they find him at the ear of Eve, tempt-
ing her in a dream, and bring him, though unwilling, to
Gabriel; by whom questioned, he scornfully answers;
prepares resistance; but hindered by a sign from
heaven, flies out of Paradise.

*

So on he fares, and to the border comes
Of Eden, where delicious Paradise,
Now nearer, crowns with her enclosure green,
As with a rural mound, the champaign head
Of a steep wilderness, whose hairy sides
With thicket overgrown, grotesque and wild,
Access denied; and overhead up-grew
Insuperable height of loftiest shade,
Cedar, and pine, and fir, and branching palm,
A sylvan scene, and as the ranks ascend
Shade above shade, a woody theatre
Of stateliest view. Yet higher than their tops
The verdurous wall of Paradise up-sprung;
Which to our general sire gave prospect large
Into his nether empire neighbouring round.

And higher than that wall a circling row
Of goodliest trees, loaded with fairest fruit,
Blossoms and fruits at once of golden hue,
Appeared, with gay enamelled colours mixed;
On which the sun more glad impressed his beams
Than in fair evening cloud, or humid bow,
When God hath showered the earth: so lovely seemed
That landscape; and of pure now purer air
Meets his approach, and to the heart inspires
Vernal delight and joy, able to drive
All sadness but despair; now gentle gales,
Fanning their odoriferous wings, dispense
Native perfumes, and whisper whence they stole
Those balmy spoils.

(Lines 131–159)

*

Now to the ascent of that steep savage hill
Satan had journeyed on, pensive and slow;
But further way found none, so thick entwined,
As one continued brake, the undergrowth
Of shrubs and tangling bushes had perplexed
All path of man or beast that passed that way;
One gate there only was, and that looked east
On the other side: which when the arch-felon saw,
Due entrance he disdained, and, in contempt,

At one slight bound high overleaped all bound
Of hill or highest wall, and sheer within
Lights on his feet. As when a prowling wolf,
Whom hunger drives to seek new haunt for prey,
Watching where shepherds pen their flocks at eve,
In hurdled cotes amid the field secure,
Leaps o'er the fence with ease into the fold;
Or as a thief, bent to unhoard the cash
Of some rich burgher, whose substantial doors,
Cross-barred and bolted fast, fear no assault,
In at the window climbs, or o'er the tiles;
So clomb this first grand thief into God's fold:
So since into his church lewd hirelings climb.
Thence up he flew, and on the tree of life,
The middle tree and highest there that grew,
Sat like a cormorant; yet not true life
Thereby regained, but sat devising death
To them who lived; nor on the virtue thought
Of that life-giving plant, but only used
For prospect, what well used had been the pledge
Of immortality. So little knows
Any, but God alone, to value right
The good before him, but perverts best things
To worst abuse, or to their meanest use.
Beneath him, with new wonder, now he views,
To all delight of human sense exposed,
In narrow room nature's whole wealth; yea, more –

A heaven on earth: for blissful Paradise
Of God the garden was, by him in the east
Of Eden planted; Eden stretched her line
From Auran eastward to the royal towers
Of great Seleucia, built by Grecian kings,
Or where the sons of Eden long before
Dwelt in Telassar; in this pleasant soil
His far more pleasant garden God ordained;
Out of the fertile ground he caused to grow
All trees of noblest kind for sight, smell, taste;
And all amid them stood the tree of life,
High eminent, blooming ambrosial fruit
Of vegetable gold; and next to life,
Our death, the tree of knowledge, grew fast by –
Knowledge of good, bought dear by knowing ill.
Southward through Eden went a river large,
Nor changed his course, but through the shaggy hill
Passed underneath ingulfed; for God had thrown
That mountain, as his garden-mould, high raised
Upon the rapid current, which through veins
Of porous earth with kindly thirst up-drawn,
Rose a fresh fountain, and with many a rill
Watered the garden; thence united fell
Down the steep glade, and met the nether flood,
Which from his darksome passage now appears,
And now, divided into four main streams,
Runs diverse, wandering many a famous realm

And country whereof here needs no account;
But rather to tell how, if art could tell
How, from that sapphire fount the crispèd brooks,
Rolling on orient pearl and sands of gold,
With mazy error under pendant shades
Ran nectar, visiting each plant, and fed
Flowers worthy of Paradise, which not nice art
In beds and curious knots, but nature boon
Poured forth profuse on hill and dale and plain,
Both where the morning sun first warmly smote
The open field, and where the unpierced shade
Embrowned the noontide bowers; thus was this place,
A happy rural seat of various view:
Groves whose rich trees wept odorous gums and balm;
Others whose fruit, burnished with golden rind,
Hung amiable – Hesperian fables true,
If true, here only – and of delicious taste;
Betwixt them lawns, or level downs, and flocks
Grazing the tender herb, were interposed,
Or palmy hillock; or the flowery lap
Of some irriguous valley spread her store,
Flowers of all hue, and without thorn the rose.
Another side, umbrageous grots and caves
Of cool recess, o'er which the mantling vine
Lays forth her purple grape, and gently creeps
Luxuriant; meanwhile murmuring waters fall
Down the slope hills dispersed, or in a lake,

That to the fringèd bank with myrtle crowned
Her crystal mirror holds, unite their streams.
The birds their choir apply; airs, vernal airs,
Breathing the smell of field and grove, attune
The trembling leaves, while universal Pan,
Knit with the Graces and the Hours in dance,
Led on the eternal Spring. Not that fair field
Of Enna, where Prosperpine gathering flowers,
Herself a fairer flower, by gloomy Dis
Was gathered – which cost Ceres all that pain
To seek her through the world – nor that sweet grove
Of Daphne, by Orontes and the inspired
Castalian spring, might with this Paradise
Of Eden strive; nor that Nyseian isle,
Girt with the river Triton, where old Cham,
Whom Gentiles Ammon call and Libyan Jove,
Hid Amalthea and her florid son,
Young Bacchus, from his stepdame Rhea's eye;
Nor, where Abassin kings their issue guard,
Mount Amara – though this by some supposed
True Paradise – under the Ethiop line
By Nilus' head, enclosed with shining rock,
A whole day's journey high, but wide remote
From this Assyrian garden, where the fiend
Saw undelighted all delight, all kind
Of living creatures, new to sight and strange.
Two of far nobler shape, erect and tall,

God-like erect, with native honour clad
In naked majesty, seemed lords of all,
And worthy seemed; for in their looks divine
The image of their glorious maker shone,
Truth, wisdom, sanctitude severe and pure –
Severe, but in true filial freedom placed,
Whence true authority in men: though both
Not equal, as their sex not equal seemed;
For contemplation he and valour formed,
For softness she and sweet attractive grace;
He for God only, she for God in him;
His fair large front and eye sublime declared
Absolute rule; and hyacinthine locks
Round from his parted forelock manly hung
Clustering, but not beneath his shoulders broad:
She as a veil down to the slender waist,
Her unadornèd golden tresses wore
Dishevelled, but in wanton ringlets waved
As the vine curls her tendrils – which implied
Subjection, but required with gentle sway,
And by her yielded, by him best received
Yielded, with coy submission, modest pride,
And sweet reluctant amorous delay.
Nor those mysterious parts were then concealed;
Then was not guilty shame, dishonest shame
Of nature's works, honour dishonourable,
Sin-bred, how have ye troubled all mankind

With shows instead, mere shows of seeming pure,
And banished from man's life his happiest life,
Simplicity and spotless innocence.
So passed they naked on, nor shunned the sight
Of God or angel, for they thought no ill:
So hand in hand they passed, the liveliest pair
That ever since in love's embraces met –
Adam the goodliest man of men since born
His sons; the fairest of her daughters Eve.

(Lines 172–324)

*

'Sole partner and sole part of all these joys,
Dearer thyself than all, needs must the power
That made us, and for us this ample world,
Be infinitely good, and of his good
As liberal and free as infinite;
That raised us from the dust, and placed us here
In all this happiness, who at his hand
Have nothing merited, nor can perform
Aught whereof he hath need; he who requires
From us no other service than to keep
This one, this easy charge – of all the trees
In Paradise that bear delicious fruit
So various, not to taste that only tree
Of knowledge, planted by the tree of life;

So near grows death to life, whate'er death is –
Some dreadful thing no doubt; for well thou know'st
God hath pronounced it death to taste that tree:
The only sign of our obedience left
Among so many signs of power and rule
Conferred upon us, and dominion given
Over all other creatures that possess
Earth, air, and sea. Then let us not think hard
One easy prohibition, who enjoy
Free leave so large to all things else, and choice
Unlimited of manifold delights;
But let us ever praise him, and extol
His bounty, following our delightful task,
To prune these growing plants, and tend these flowers;
Which, were it toilsome, yet with thee were sweet.'
    To whom thus Eve replied: 'O thou for whom
And from whom I was formed flesh of thy flesh,
And without whom am to no end, my guide
And head, what thou hast said is just and right.
For we to him indeed all praises owe,
And daily thanks – I chiefly, who enjoy
So far the happier lot, enjoying thee
Pre-eminent by so much odds, while thou
Like consort to thyself canst nowhere find.
That day I oft remember, when from sleep
I first awaked, and found myself reposed,
Under a shade on flowers, much wondering where

And what I was, whence thither brought, and how.
Not distant far from thence a murmuring sound
Of waters issued from a cave, and spread
Into a liquid plain, then stood unmoved,
Pure as the expanse of heaven; I thither went
With unexperienced thought, and laid me down
On the green bank, to look into the clear
Smooth lake, that to me seemed another sky.
As I bent down to look, just opposite
A shape within the watery gleam appeared,
Bending to look on me; I started back,
It started back, but pleased I soon returned,
Pleased it returned as soon with answering looks
Of sympathy and love; there I had fixed
Mine eyes till now, and pined with vain desire,
Had not a voice thus warned me: "What thou seest,
What there thou seest, fair creature, is thyself:
With thee it came and goes: but follow me,
And I will bring thee where no shadow stays
Thy coming, and thy soft embraces – he
Whose image thou art; him thou shalt enjoy
Inseparably thine; to him shalt bear
Multitudes like thyself, and thence be called
Mother of human race"; what could I do,
But follow straight, invisibly thus led?
Till I espied thee, fair indeed and tall,
Under a platan; yet methought less fair,

Less winning soft, less amiably mild,
Than that smooth watery image; back I turned;
Thou, following, cried'st aloud, "Return, fair Eve;
Whom fliest thou? Whom thou fliest, of him thou art,
His flesh, his bone; to give thee being I lent
Out of my side to thee, nearest my heart,
Substantial life, to have thee by my side
Henceforth an individual solace dear:
Part of my soul I seek thee, and thee claim
My other half"; with that thy gentle hand
Seized mine: I yielded, and from that time see
How beauty is excelled by manly grace
And wisdom, which alone is truly fair.'

(Lines 411–491)

*

Thus talking, hand in hand alone they passed
On to their blissful bower; it was a place
Chosen by the sovereign planter, when he framed
All things to man's delightful use; the roof
Of thickest covert was inwoven shade,
Laurel and myrtle, and what higher grew
Of firm and fragrant leaf; on either side
Acanthus, and each odorous bushy shrub,
Fenced up the verdant wall; each beauteous flower,
Iris all hues, roses, and jessamine,

Reared high their flourished heads between, and
      wrought
Mosaic; under foot the violet,
Crocus, and hyacinth, with rich inlay
Broidered the ground, more coloured than with stone
Of costliest emblem; other creature here,
Beast, bird, insect, or worm, durst enter none;
Such was their awe of man. In shadier bower
More sacred and sequestered, though but feigned,
Pan or Sylvanus never slept, nor nymph
Nor Faunus haunted. Here, in close recess,
With flowers, garlands, and sweet-smelling herbs,
Espousèd Eve decked her first nuptial bed.
And heavenly choirs the hymenean sung,
What day the genial angel to our sire
Brought her, in naked beauty more adorned,
More lovely than Pandora, whom the gods
Endowed with all their gifts; and, O too like
In sad event, when to the unwiser son
Of Japhet brought by Hermes, she ensnared
Mankind with her fair looks, to be avenged
On him who had stole Jove's authentic fire.

    Thus at their shady lodge arrived, both stood,
Both turned, and under open sky adored
The God that made both sky, air, earth and heaven,
Which they beheld, the moon's resplendent globe,
And starry pole: 'Thou also madest the night,

Maker omnipotent; and thou the day,
Which we in our appointed work employed,
Have finished, happy in our mutual help
And mutual love, the crown of all our bliss
Ordained by thee; and this delicious place,
For us too large, where thy abundance wants
Partakers, and uncropped falls to the ground.
But thou hast promised from us two a race
To fill the earth, who shall with us extol
Thy goodness infinite, both when we wake,
And when we seek, as now, thy gift of sleep.'
    This said unanimous, and other rites
Observing none, but adoration pure,
Which God likes best, into their inmost bower
Handed they went; and, eased the putting-off
These troublesome disguises which we wear,
Straight side by side were laid; nor turned, I ween,
Adam from his fair spouse, nor Eve the rites
Mysterious of connubial love refused:
Whatever hypocrites austerely talk
Of purity, and place, and innocence,
Defaming as impure what God declares
Pure, and commands to some, leaves free to all.
Our maker bids increase; who bids abstain
But our destroyer, foe to God and man?
Hail, wedded love, mysterious law, true source
Of human offspring, sole propriety

In Paradise of all things common else.
By thee adulterous lust was driven from men
Among the bestial herds to range; by thee,
Founded in reason, loyal, just, and pure
Relations dear, and all the charities
Of father, son, and brother, first were known.
Far be it that I should write thee sin or blame,
Or think thee unbefitting holiest place,
Perpetual fountain of domestic sweets,
Whose bed is undefiled and chaste pronounced,
Present, or past, as saints and patriarchs used.
Here Love his golden shafts employs, here lights
His constant lamp, and waves his purple wings,
Reigns here and revels; not in the bought smile
Of harlots – loveless, joyless, unendeared,
Casual fruition; nor in court amours,
Mixed dance, or wanton mask, or midnight ball,
Or serenade, which the starved lover sings
To his proud fair, best quitted with disdain.
These, lulled by nightingales, embracing slept,
And on their naked limbs the flowery roof
Showered roses, which the morn repaired. Sleep on,
Blest pair; and O yet happiest if ye seek
No happier state, and know to know no more.

(Lines 689–775)

BOOK V

Morning approached, Eve relates to Adam her trouble-
some dream; he likes it not, yet comforts her; they
come forth to their day labours: their morning hymn
at the door of their bower. God, to render man
inexcusable, sends Raphael to admonish him of his
obedience, of his free estate, of his enemy near at hand,
who he is, and why his enemy, and whatever else may
avail Adam to know. Raphael comes down to Paradise;
his appearance described; his coming discerned by
Adam afar off, sitting at the door of his bower; he goes
out to meet him, brings him to his lodge, entertains
him with the choicest fruits of Paradise, got together
by Eve; their discourse at table. Raphael performs his
message, minds Adam of his state and of his enemy;
relates, at Adam's request, who that enemy is, and
how he came to be so, beginning from his first revolt
in heaven, and the occasion thereof; how he drew his
legions after him to the parts of the north, and there
incited them to rebel with him, persuading all but
only Abdiel, a seraph, who in argument dissuades and
opposes him, then forsakes him.

Now Morn, her rosy steps in the eastern clime
Advancing, sowed the earth with orient pearl,
When Adam waked, so customed; for his sleep
Was airy light, from pure digestion bred,
And temperate vapours bland, which the only sound
Of leaves and fuming rills, Aurora's fan,
Lightly dispersed, and the shrill matin song
Of birds on every bough; so much the more
His wonder was to find unwakened Eve,
With tresses discomposed, and glowing cheek,
As through unquiet rest; he on his side
Leaning half raised, with looks of cordial love
Hung over her enamoured, and beheld
Beauty which, whether waking or asleep,
Shot forth peculiar graces; then with voice
Mild as when Zephyrus on Flora breathes,
Her hand soft touching, whispered thus: 'Awake,
My fairest, my espoused, my latest found,
Heaven's last, best gift, my ever-new delight;
Awake, the morning shines, and the fresh field
Calls us; we lose the prime to mark how spring
Our tended plants, how blows the citron grove,
What drops the myrrh, and what the balmy reed,
How nature paints her colours, how the bee
Sits on the bloom extracting liquid sweet.'
   Such whispering waked her, but with startled eye
On Adam; whom embracing, thus she spake:

'O sole in whom my thoughts find all repose,
My glory, my perfection, glad I see
Thy face, and morn returned; for I this night –
Such night till this I never passed – have dreamed,
If dreamed, not as I oft am wont, of thee,
Works of day past, or morrow's next design,
But of offence and trouble, which my mind
Knew never till this irksome night; methought
Close at mine ear one called me forth to walk
With gentle voice; I thought it thine; it said,
"Why sleep'st thou, Eve? Now is the pleasant time,
The cool, the silent, save where silence yields
To the night-warbling bird, that now awake
Tunes sweetest his love-laboured song; now reigns
Full-orbed the moon, and with more pleasing light,
Shadowy sets off the face of things – in vain,
If none regard; heaven wakes with all his eyes,
Whom to behold but thee, nature's desire,
In whose sight all things joy, with ravishment
Attracted by thy beauty still to gaze?"
I rose as at thy call, but found thee not:
To find thee I directed then my walk;
And on, methought, alone I passed through ways
That brought me on a sudden to the tree
Of interdicted knowledge; fair it seemed,
Much fairer to my fancy than by day;
And as I wondering looked, beside it stood

One shaped and winged like one of those from heaven
By us oft seen: his dewy locks distilled
Ambrosia; on that tree he also gazed;
And, "O fair plant," said he, "with fruit surcharged,
Deigns none to ease thy load and taste thy sweet,
Nor God nor man? Is knowledge so despised?
Or envy, or what reserve forbids to taste?
Forbid who will, none shall from me withhold
Longer thy offered good, why else set here?"
This said, he paused not, but with venturous arm
He plucked, he tasted; me damp horror chilled
At such bold words vouched with a deed so bold;
But he thus, overjoyed: "O fruit divine,
Sweet of thyself, but much more sweet thus cropped,
Forbidden here, it seems, as only fit
For gods, yet able to make gods of men;
And why not gods of men, since good, the more
Communicated, more abundant grows,
The author not impaired, but honoured more?
Here, happy creature, fair angelic Eve,
Partake thou also: happy though thou art,
Happier thou may'st be, worthier canst not be;
Taste this, and be henceforth among the gods
Thyself a goddess, not to earth confined,
But sometimes in the air, as we; sometimes
Ascend to heaven, by merit thine, and see
What life the gods live there, and such live thou."

So saying, he drew nigh, and to me held,
Even to my mouth of that same fruit held part
Which he had plucked: the pleasant savoury smell
So quickened appetite that I, methought,
Could not but taste. Forthwith up to the clouds
With him I flew, and underneath beheld
The earth outstretched immense, a prospect wide
And various; wondering at my flight and change
To this high exaltation, suddenly
My guide was gone, and I, methought, sunk down,
And fell asleep; but O how glad I waked
To find this but a dream!' Thus Eve her night
Related, and thus Adam answered sad:

   'Best image of myself and dearer half,
The trouble of thy thoughts this night in sleep
Affects me equally; nor can I like
This uncouth dream – of evil sprung, I fear;
Yet evil whence? In thee can harbour none,
Created pure. But know that in the soul
Are many lesser faculties that serve
Reason as chief; among these Fancy next
Her office holds; of all external things,
Which the five watchful senses represent,
She forms imaginations, airy shapes,
Which Reason, joining or disjoining, frames
All what we affirm or what deny, and call
Our knowledge or opinion; then retires

Into her private cell when nature rests.
Oft, in her absence, mimic Fancy wakes
To imitate her; but, misjoining shapes,
Wild work produces oft, and most in dreams,
Ill matching words and deeds long past or late.
Some such resemblances methinks I find
Of our last evening's talk in this thy dream,
But with addition strange; yet be not sad.
Evil into the mind of god or man
May come and go, so unapproved, and leave
No spot or blame behind; which gives me hope
That what in sleep thou did'st abhor to dream
Waking thou never wilt consent to do.
Be not disheartened then, nor cloud those looks,
That wont to be more cheerful and serene
Than when fair morning first smiles on the world;
And let us to our fresh employments rise
Among the groves, the fountains, and the flowers,
That open now their choicest bosomed smells,
Reserved from night, and kept for thee in store.'
   So cheered he his fair spouse; and she was cheered,
But silently a gentle tear let fall
From either eye, and wiped them with her hair:
Two other precious drops that ready stood,
Each in their crystal sluice, he, ere they fell,
Kissed as the gracious signs of sweet remorse
And pious awe, that feared to have offended.
(Lines 1–135)

'Hail mother of mankind, whose fruitful womb
Shall fill the world more numerous with thy sons
Than with these various fruits the trees of God
Have heaped this table.' Raised of grassy turf
Their table was, and mossy seats had round,
And on her ample square, from side to side,
All autumn piled, though spring and autumn here
Danced hand-in-hand. A while discourse they hold –
No fear lest dinner cool – when thus began
Our author: 'Heavenly stranger, please to taste
These bounties, which our nourisher, from whom
All perfect good, unmeasured-out, descends,
To us for food and for delight hath caused
The earth to yield: unsavoury food, perhaps,
To spiritual natures; only this I know,
That one celestial Father gives to all.'
    To whom the angel: 'Therefore, what he gives
(Whose praise be ever sung) to man, in part
Spiritual, may of purest spirits be found
No ingrateful food: and food alike those pure
Intelligential substances require
As doth your rational; and both contain
Within them every lower faculty
Of sense, whereby they hear, see, smell, touch, taste,
Tasting concoct, digest, assimilate,
And corporeal to incorporeal turn.
For know, whatever was created needs

To be sustained and fed; of elements
The grosser feeds the purer: earth the sea;
Earth and the sea feed air; the air those fires
Ethereal, and, as lowest, first the moon;
Whence in her visage round those spots, unpurged
Vapours not yet into her substance turned.
Nor doth the moon no nourishment exhale
From her moist continent to higher orbs.
The sun, that light imparts to all, receives
From all his alimental recompense
In humid exhalations, and at even
Sups with the ocean; though in heaven the trees
Of life ambrosial fruitage bear, and vines
Yield nectar – though from off the boughs each morn
We brush mellifluous dews and find the ground
Covered with pearly grain – yet God hath here
Varied his bounty so with new delights
As may compare with heaven; and to taste
Think not I shall be nice.' So down they sat,
And to their viands fell, nor seemingly
The angel, nor in mist – the common gloss
Of theologians – but with keen dispatch
Of real hunger, and concoctive heat
To transubstantiate: what redounds transpires
Through spirits with ease; nor wonder, if by fire
Of sooty coal the empiric alchemist
Can turn, or holds it possible to turn,

Metals of drossiest ore to perfect gold,
As from the mine. Meanwhile at table Eve
Ministered naked, and their flowing cups
With pleasant liquors crowned: O innocence
Deserving Paradise! If ever, then,
Then had the sons of God excuse to have been
Enamoured at that sight. But in those hearts
Love unlibidinous reigned, nor jealousy
Was understood, the injured lover's hell.

(Lines 388–450)

BOOK VI

THE ARGUMENT

Raphael continues to relate how Michael and Gabriel were sent forth to battle against Satan and his angels. The first fight described: Satan and his powers retire under night; he calls a council; invents devilish engines, which, in the second day's fight, put Michael and his angels to some disorder; but they at length, pulling up mountains, overwhelmed both the force and machines of Satan. Yet, the tumult not so ending, God, on the third day, sends Messiah his Son, for whom he had reserved the glory of that victory; he, in the power of his Father, coming to the place, and causing all his legions to stand still on either side, with his chariot and thunder driving into the midst of his enemies pursued them, unable to resist, towards the wall of heaven; which opening, they leap down with horror and confusion into the place of punishment prepared for them in the deep. Messiah returns with triumph to his Father.

*

'They ended parle, and both addressed for fight
Unspeakable; for who, though with the tongue
Of angels, can relate, or to what things;
Liken on earth conspicuous, that may lift
Human imagination to such height

Of godlike power? For likest gods they seemed,
Stood they or moved, in stature, motion, arms,
Fit to decide the empire of great heaven.
Now waved their fiery swords, and in the air
Made horrid circles; two broad suns their shields
Blazed opposite, while Expectation stood
In horror; from each hand with speed retired,
Where erst was thickest fight, the angelic throng,
And left large field, unsafe within the wind
Of such commotion: such as – to set forth
Great things by small – if, nature's concord broke,
Among the constellations war were sprung,
Two planets, rushing from aspéct malign
Of fiercest opposition, in mid sky
Should combat, and their jarring spheres confound
Together both, with next to almighty arm
Uplifted imminent, one stroke they aimed
That might determine, and not need repeat
As not of power, at once; nor odds appeared
In might or swift prevention; but the sword
Of Michael from the armoury of God
Was given him tempered so, that neither keen
Nor solid might resist that edge: it met
The sword of Satan with steep force to smite
Descending, and in half cut sheer; nor stayed,
But, with swift wheel reverse, deep entering, shared
All his right side; then Satan first knew pain,

And writhed him to and fro convolved; so sore
The griding sword with discontinuous wound
Passed through him; but the ethereal substance closed,
Not long divisible, and from the gash
A stream of nectarous humour issuing flowed
Sanguine, such as celestial spirits may bleed,
And all his armour stained, erewhile so bright.
Forthwith, on all sides, to his aid was run
By angels many and strong, who interposed
Defence, while others bore him on their shields
Back to his chariot where it stood retired
From off the files of war: there they him laid
Gnashing for anguish, and despite, and shame
To find himself not matchless, and his pride
Humbled by such rebuke, so far beneath
His confidence to equal God in power.
Yet soon he healed; for spirits, that live throughout
Vital in every part – not, as frail man,
In entrails, heart or head, liver or reins –
Cannot but by annihilating die;
Nor in their liquid texture mortal wound
Receive, no more than can the fluid air:
All heart they live, all head, all eye, all ear,
All intellect, all sense; and as they please
They limb themselves, and colour, shape, or size
Assume, as likes them best, condense or rare.

(Lines 296–353)

The invention all admired, and each how he
To be the inventor missed; so easy it seemed
Once found, which yet unfound most would have thought
Impossible; yet haply of thy race,
In future days, if malice should abound,
Some one, intent on mischief, or inspired
With devilish machination, might devise
Like instrument to plague the sons of men
For sin, on war and mutual slaughter bent.
Forthwith from council to the work they flew;
None arguing stood; innumerable hands
Were ready; in a moment up they turned
Wide the celestial soil, and saw beneath
The originals of nature in their crude
Conception; sulphurous and nitrous foam
They found, they mingled, and with subtle art
Concocted and adusted, they reduced
To blackest grain, and into store conveyed;
Part hidden veins digged up (nor hath this earth
Entrails unlike) of mineral and stone,
Whereof to found their engines and their balls
Of missive ruin; part incentive reed
Provide, pernicious with one touch to fire.
So all ere day-spring, under conscious night,
Secret they finished, and in order set,
With silent circumspection, unespied.

(Lines 498–523)

'"Stand still in bright array, ye saints; here stand,
Ye angels armed; this day from battle rest;
Faithful hath been your warfare, and of God
Accepted, fearless in his righteous cause;
And as ye have received, so have ye done,
Invincibly; but of this cursed crew
The punishment to other hand belongs;
Vengeance is his, or whose he sole appoints;
Number to this day's work is not ordained,
Nor multitude; stand only and behold
God's indignation on these godless poured
By me; not you, but me, they have despised,
Yet envied; against me is all their rage,
Because the Father, to whom in heaven supreme
Kingdom and power and glory appertains,
Hath honoured me according to his will.
Therefore to me their doom he hath assigned,
That they may have their wish, to try with me
In battle which the stronger proves – they all,
Or I alone against them; since by strength
They measure all, of other excellence
Not emulous, nor care who them excels;
Nor other strife with them do I vouchsafe."
'So spake the Son, and into terror changed
His countenance, too severe to be beheld,
And full of wrath bent on his enemies.
At once the four spread out their starry wings

With dreadful shade contiguous, and the orbs
Of his fierce chariot rolled, as with the sound
Of torrent floods, or of a numerous host.
He on his impious foes right onward drove,
Gloomy as night; under his burning wheels
The steadfast empyrean shook throughout,
All but the throne itself of God. Full soon
Among them he arrived, in his right hand
Grasping ten thousand thunders, which he sent
Before him, such as in their souls infixed
Plagues. They, astonished, all resistance lost,
All courage; down their idle weapons dropped;
O'er shields, and helms, and helmed heads he rode
Of thrones and mighty seraphim prostráte,
That wished the mountains now might be again
Thrown on them, as a shelter from his ire.
Nor less on either side tempestuous fell
His arrows, from the fourfold-visaged four,
Distinct with eyes, and from the living wheels,
Distinct alike with multitude of eyes;
One spirit in them ruled, and every eye
Glared lightning, and shot forth pernicious fire
Among the accursed, that withered all their strength,
And of their wonted vigour left them drained,
Exhausted, spiritless, afflicted, fallen.
Yet half his strength he put not forth, but checked
His thunder in mid-volley; for he meant

Not to destroy, but root them out of heaven;
The overthrown he raised, and as a herd
Of goats or timorous flock together thronged,
Drove them before him thunderstruck, pursued
With terrors and with furies to the bounds
And crystal wall of heaven, which, opening wide,
Rolled inward, and a spacious gap disclosed
Into the wasteful deep; the monstrous sight
Strook them with horror backward; but far worse
Urged them behind: headlong themselves they threw
Down from the verge of heaven: eternal wrath
Burnt after them to the bottomless pit.
  'Hell heard the unsufferable noise; hell saw
Heaven ruining from heaven, and would have fled
Affrighted; but strict fate had cast too deep
Her dark foundations, and too fast had bound.
Nine days they fell; confounded Chaos roared,
And felt tenfold confusion in their fall
Through his wild anarchy; so huge a rout
Encumbered him with ruin; hell at last,
Yawning, received them whole, and on them closed –
Hell, their fit habitation, fraught with fire
Unquenchable, the house of woe and pain.
Disburdened heaven rejoiced, and soon repaired
Her mural breach, returning whence it rolled.
Sole victor, from the expulsion of his foes
Messiah his triumphal chariot turned;

To meet him all his saints, who silent stood
Eye-witnesses of his almighty acts,
With jubilee advanced; and as they went,
Shaded with branching palm, each order bright
Sung triumph, and him sung victorious king,
Son, heir, and Lord, to him dominion given,
Worthiest to reign; he celebrated rode,
Triumphant through mid heaven, into the courts
And temple of his mighty Father throned
On high; who into glory him received,
Where now he sits at the right hand of bliss.
   Thus, measuring things in heaven by things
      on earth,
At thy request, and that thou may'st beware
By what is past, to thee I have revealed
What might have else to human race been hid –
The discord which befell, and war in heaven
Among the angelic powers, and the deep fall
Of those too high aspiring who rebelled
With Satan: he who envies now thy state,
Who now is plotting how he may seduce
Thee also from obedience, that with him
Bereaved of happiness, thou may'st partake
His punishment, eternal misery;
Which would be all his solace and revenge,
As a despite done against the most high,
Thee once to gain companion of his woe.

But listen not to his temptations; warn
Thy weaker; let it profit thee to have heard,
By terrible example, the reward
Of disobedience; firm they might have stood,
Yet fell; remember, and fear to transgress.'

(Lines 801–912)

BOOK VII

Raphael, at the request of Adam, relates how and
wherefore this world was first created: that God, after
the expelling of Satan and his angels out of heaven,
declared his pleasure to create another world, and
other creatures to dwell therein; sends his Son with
glory, and attendance of angels, to perform the work
of creation in six days: the angels celebrate with
hymns the performance thereof, and his reascension
into heaven.

*

On heavenly ground they stood, and from the shore
They viewed the vast immeasurable abyss,
Outrageous as a sea, dark, wasteful, wild,
Up from the bottom turned by furious winds
And surging waves, as mountains to assault
Heaven's height, and with the centre mix the pole.
  ' "Silence, ye troubled waves, and thou deep, peace,"
Said then the omnific Word: "Your discord end;"
Nor stayed, but, on the wings of cherubim
Uplifted, in paternal glory rode
Far into chaos and the world unborn;
For chaos heard his voice; him all his train
Followed in bright procession to behold

Creation and the wonders of his might.
Then stayed the fervid wheels, and in his hand
He took the golden compasses, prepared
In God's eternal store, to circumscribe
This universe, and all created things;
One foot he centred, and the other turned
Round through the vast profundity obscure,
And said, "Thus far extend, thus far thy bounds;
This be thy just circumference, O world."
Thus God the heaven created, thus the earth,
Matter unformed and void; darkness profound
Covered the abyss; but on the watery calm
His brooding wings the spirit of God outspread,
And vital virtue infused, and vital warmth,
Throughout the fluid mass, but downward purged
The black tartareous cold infernal dregs,
Adverse to life; then founded, then conglobed,
Like things to like, the rest to several place
Disparted, and between spun out the air,
And earth, self-balanced, on her centre hung.
  ' "Let there be light," said God, and forthwith light
Ethereal, first of things, quintessence pure,
Sprung from the deep, and from her native east
To journey through the airy gloom began,
Sphered in a radiant cloud – for yet the sun
Was not; she in a cloudy tabernacle
Sojourned the while. God saw the light was good;

And light from darkness by the hemisphere
Divided: light the day, and darkness night,
He named. Thus was the first day even and morn;
Nor passed uncelebrated, nor unsung
By the celestial choirs, when orient light
Exhaling first from darkness they beheld,
Birth-day of heaven and earth; with joy and shout
The hollow universal orb they filled,
And touched their golden harps, and hymning praised
God and his works; creator him they sung,
Both when first evening was, and when first morn.
    'Again God said, "Let there be firmament
Amid the waters, and let it divide
The waters from the waters"; and God made
The firmament, expanse of liquid, pure,
Transparent, elemental air diffused
In circuit to the uttermost convex
Of this great round – partition firm and sure,
The waters underneath from those above
Dividing; for as earth, so he the world
Built on circumfluous waters calm, in wide
Crystalline ocean, and the loud misrule
Of chaos far removed, lest fierce extremes
Contiguous might distemper the whole frame:
And heaven he named the firmament; so even
And morning chorus sung the second day.
    'The earth was formed, but in the womb as yet

Of waters, embryon immature, involved,
Appeared not; over all the face of earth
Main ocean flowed, not idle, but with warm
Prolific humous softening all her globe,
Fermented the great mother to conceive,
Satiate with genial moisture; when God said,
"Be gathered now, ye waters under heaven,
Into one place, and let dry land appear."
Immediately the mountains huge appear
Emergent, and their broad bare backs upheave
Into the clouds; their tops ascend the sky;
So high as heaved the tumid hills, so low
Down sunk a hollow bottom broad and deep,
Capacious bed of waters; thither they
Hasted with glad precipitance, uprolled
As drops on dust conglobing from the dry:
Part rise in crystal wall, or ridge direct,
For haste; such flight the great command impressed
On the swift floods; as armies at the call
Of trumpet (for of armies thou hast heard)
Troop to their standard, so the watery throng,
Wave rolling after wave, where way they found –
If steep, with torrent rapture, if through plain,
Soft-ebbing; nor withstood them rock or hill;
But they, or underground, or circuit wide
With serpent error wandering, found their way,
And on the washy ooze deep channels wore:

Easy, ere God had bid the ground be dry,
All but within those banks where rivers now
Stream, and perpetual draw their humid train.
The dry land earth, and the great receptacle
Of congregated waters he called seas;
And saw that it was good, and said, "Let the earth
Put forth the verdant grass, herb yielding seed,
And fruit-tree yielding fruit after her kind,
Whose seed is in herself upon the earth."
He scarce had said when the bare earth, till then
Desert and bare, unsightly, unadorned,
Brought forth the tender grass, whose verdure clad
Her universal face with pleasant green;
Then herbs of every leaf, that sudden flowered,
Opening their various colours, and made gay
Her bosom, smelling sweet; and these scarce blown,
Forth flourished thick the clustering vine, forth crept
The swelling gourd, up stood the corny reed
Embattled in her field: and the humble shrub,
And bush with frizzled hair implicit: last
Rose, as in dance, the stately trees, and spread
Their branches hung with copious fruit, or gemmed
Their blossoms; with high woods the hills were crowned,
With tufts the valleys and each fountain-side,
With borders long the rivers, that earth now
Seemed like to heaven, a seat where gods might dwell,
Or wander with delight, and love to haunt

Her sacred shades; though God had yet not rained
Upon the earth, and man to till the ground
None was, but from the earth a dewy mist
Went up and watered all the ground, and each
Plant of the field, which ere it was in the earth
God made, and every herb before it grew
On the green stem; God saw that it was good;
So even and morn recorded the third day.

    'Again the almighty spake, "Let there be lights
High in the expanse of heaven, to divide
The day from night; and let them be for signs,
For seasons, and for days, and circling years;
And let them be for lights, as I ordain
Their office in the firmament of heaven,
To give light on the earth;" and it was so.
And God made two great lights, great for their use
To man, the greater to have rule by day,
The less by night, altern; and made the stars,
And set them in the firmament of heaven
To illuminate the earth, and rule the day
In their vicissitude, and rule the night,
And light from darkness to divide. God saw,
Surveying his great work, that it was good:
For, of celestial bodies, first the sun
A mighty sphere he framed, unlightsome first,
Though of ethereal mould; then formed the moon
Globose, and every magnitude of stars,

And sowed with stars the heaven thick as a field;
Of light by far the greater part he took,
Transplanted from her cloudy shrine, and placed
In the sun's orb, made porous to receive
And drink the liquid light, firm to retain
Her gathered beams, great palace now of light.
Hither, as to their fountain, other stars
Repairing in their golden urns draw light.
And hence the morning planet gilds her horns;
By tincture or reflection they augment
Their small peculiar, though, from human sight
So far remote, with diminution seen.
First in his east the glorious lamp was seen,
Regent of day, and all the horizon round
Invested with bright rays, jocund to run
His longitude through heaven's high road; the grey
Dawn, and the Pleiades before him danced,
Shedding sweet influence; less bright the moon,
But opposite in levelled west, was set,
His mirror, with full face borrowing her light
From him, for other light she needed none
In that aspect, and still that distance keeps
Till night; then in the east her turn she shines,
Revolved on heaven's great axle, and her reign
With thousand lesser lights dividual holds,
With thousand thousand stars, that then appeared
Spangling the hemisphere; then first adorned

With their bright luminaries, that set and rose,
Glad evening and glad morn crowned the fourth day.
    'And God said, "Let the waters generate
Reptile with spawn abundant, living soul;
And let fowl fly above the earth, with wings
Displayed on the open firmament of heaven."
And God created the great whales, and each
Soul living, each that crept, which plenteously
The waters generated by their kinds,
And every bird of wing after his kind,
And saw that it was good, and blessed them, saying,
"Be fruitful, multiply, and in the seas,
And lakes and running streams the waters fill;
And let the fowl be multiplied on the earth."
Forthwith the sounds and seas, each creek and bay,
With fry innumerable swarm, and shoals
Of fish that with their fins and shining scales
Glide under the green wave in sculls that oft
Bank the mid-sea; part, single or with mate,
Graze the sea-weed, their pasture, and through groves
Of coral stray, or sporting with quick glance
Show to the sun their waved coats dropped with gold,
Or in their pearly shells at ease, attend
Moist nutriment, or under rocks their food
In jointed armour watch; on smooth the seal
And bended dolphins play: part, huge of bulk,
Wallowing unwieldy, enormous in their gait,

Tempest the ocean; there leviathan,
Hugest of living creatures, on the deep
Stretched like a promontory, sleeps or swims,
And seems a moving land, and at his gills
Draws in, and at his trunk spouts out, a sea.
Meanwhile the tepid caves, and fens, and shores,
Their brood as numerous hatch from the egg, that soon,
Bursting with kindly rupture, forth disclosed
Their callow young; but feathered soon and fledge
They summed their pens, and soaring the air sublime,
With clang despised the ground, under a cloud
In prospect; there the eagle and the stork
On cliffs and cedar-tops their eyries build;
Part loosely wing the region; part, more wise,
In common, ranged in figure, wedge their way,
Intelligent of seasons, and set forth
Their airy caravan, high over seas
Flying, and over lands, with mutual wing
Easing their flight: so steers the prudent crane
Her annual voyage, borne on winds: the air
Floats as they pass, fanned with unnumbered plumes;
From branch to branch the smaller birds with song
Solaced the woods, and spread their painted wings,
Till even; nor then the solemn nightingale
Ceased warbling, but all night tuned her soft lays;
Others, on silver lakes and rivers, bathed
Their downy breast; the swan, with archèd neck

Between her white wings mantling proudly, rows
Her state with oary feet; yet oft they quit
The dank, and, rising on stiff pennons, tower
The mid aerial sky; others on ground
Walked firm – the crested cock, whose clarion sounds
The silent hours, and the other, whose gay train
Adorns him, coloured with the florid hue
Of rainbows and starry eyes. The waters thus
With fish replenished, and the air with fowl,
Evening and morn solemnised the fifth day.
    'The sixth, and of creation last, arose
With evening harps and matin; when God said,
"Let the earth bring forth soul living in her kind,
Cattle, and creeping things, and beast of the earth,
Each in their kind." The earth obeyed, and, straight
Opening her fertile womb, teemed at a birth
Innumerous living creatures, perfect forms,
Limbed and full-grown; out of the ground up rose,
As from his lair, the wild beast, where he wons
In forest wild, in thicket, brake, or den –
Among the trees in pairs they rose, they walked;
The cattle in the fields and meadows green:
Those rare and solitary, these in flocks
Pasturing at once and in broad herds, upsprung.
The grassy clods now calved; now half appeared
The tawny lion pawing to get free
His hinder parts – then springs, as broke from bonds,

And rampant shakes his brinded mane; the ounce,
The libbard, and the tiger, as the mole
Rising, the crumbled earth above them threw
In hillocks; the swift stag from underground
Bore up his branching head; scarce from his mould
Behemoth, biggest born of earth, upheaved
His vastness; fleeced the flocks and bleating rose,
As plants; ambiguous between sea and land,
The river-horse and scaly crocodile.
At once came forth whatever creeps the ground,
Insect or worm; those waved their limber fans
For wings, and smallest lineaments exact
In all the liveries decked of summer's pride,
With spots of gold and purple, azure and green;
These as a line their long dimension drew,
Streaking the ground with sinuous trace; not all
Minims of nature; some of serpent kind,
Wondrous in length and corpulence, involved
Their snaky folds, and added wings. First crept
The parsimonious emmet, provident
Of future, in small room large heart enclosed —
Pattern of just equality perhaps
Hereafter — joined in her popular tribes
Of commonalty; swarming next appeared
The female bee, that feeds her husband drone
Deliciously, and builds her waxen cells
With honey stored; the rest are numberless,

And thou their natures know'st, and gav'st them names,
Needless to thee repeated; nor unknown
The serpent, subtlest beast of all the field,
Of huge extent sometimes, with brazen eyes,
And hairy mane terrific, though to thee
Not noxious, but obedient at thy call.
   'Now heaven in all her glory shone, and rolled
Her motions, as the great first mover's hand
First wheeled their course; earth, in her rich attire
Consummate, lovely smiled; air, water, earth,
By fowl, fish, beast, was flown, was swum, was walked,
Frequent; and of the sixth day yet remained;
There wanted yet the master-work, the end
Of all yet done – a creature who not prone
And brute as other creatures, but endued
With sanctity of reason, might erect
His stature, and upright with front serene
Govern the rest, self-knowing, and from thence
Magnanimous to correspond with heaven,
But grateful to acknowledge whence his good
Descends; thither with heart and voice and eyes
Directed in devotion, to adore
And worship God supreme, who made him chief
Of all his works; therefore the omnipotent
Eternal Father (for where is not he
Present?) thus to his Son audibly spake:
"Let us make now man in our image, man

In our similitude, and let them rule
Over the fish and fowl of sea and air,
Beast of the field, and over all the earth,
And every creeping thing that creeps the ground."
This said, he formed thee, Adam, thee O man,
Dust of the ground, and in thy nostrils breathed
The breath of life; in his own image he
Created thee, in the image of God
Express, and thou becam'st a living soul.
Male he created thee, but thy consort
Female, for race; then blessed mankind, and said,
"Be fruitful, multiply, and fill the earth;
Subdue it, and throughout dominion hold
Over fish of the sea, and fowl of the air,
And every living thing that moves on the earth."
Wherever thus created – for no place
Is yet distinct by name – thence, as thou know'st,
He brought thee into this delicious grove,
This garden, planted with the trees of God,
Delectable both to behold and taste,
And freely all their pleasant fruit for food
Gave thee: all sorts are here that all the earth yields,
Variety without end; but of the tree
Which tasted works knowledge of good and evil
Thou may'st not; in the day thou eat'st, thou diest.
Death is the penalty imposed; beware,
And govern well thy appetite, lest Sin

Surprise thee, and her black attendant Death.
  'Here finished he, and all that he had made
Viewed, and behold all was entirely good;
So even and morn accomplished the sixth day;
Yet not till the creator from his work
Desisting, though unwearied, up returned,
Up to the heaven of heavens, his high abode,
Thence to behold this new-created world,
The addition of his empire, how it showed
In prospect from his throne, how good, how fair,
Answering his great idea. Up he rode,
Followed with acclamation, and the sound
Symphonious of ten thousand harps, that tuned
Angelic harmonies; the earth, the air
Resounded (thou remember'st, for thou heard'st),
The heavens and all the constellations rung,
The planets in their stations listening stood,
While the bright pomp ascended jubilant.

(Lines 210–564)

BOOK VIII

Adam enquires concerning celestial motions; is doubt-
fully answered, and exhorted to search rather things
more worthy of knowledge; Adam assents, and still
desirous to detain Raphael, relates to him what he
remembered since his own creation – his placing in
Paradise; his talk with God concerning solitude and
fit society; his first meeting and nuptials with Eve;
his discourse with the angel thereupon; who, after
admonitions repeated, departs.

*

Mine eyes he closed, but open left the cell
Of fancy, my internal sight, by which,
Abstract as in a trance, methought I saw,
Though sleeping, where I lay, and saw the shape
Still glorious before whom awake I stood;
Who, stooping, opened my left side, and took
From thence a rib, with cordial spirits warm,
And life-blood streaming fresh; wide was the wound,
But suddenly with flesh filled up and healed;
The rib he formed and fashioned with his hands;
Under his forming hands a creature grew,
Man-like, but different sex, so lovely fair
That what seemed fair in all the world seemed now

Mean, or in her summed up, in her contained
And in her looks, which from that time infused
Sweetness into my heart unfelt before
And into all things from her air inspired
The spirit of love and amorous delight.
She disappeared, and left me dark; I waked
To find her, or for ever to deplore
Her loss, and other pleasures all abjure:
When, out of hope, behold her not far off,
Such as I saw her in my dream, adorned
With what all earth and heaven could bestow
To make her amiable; on she came,
Led by her heavenly maker, though unseen
And guided by his voice, nor uninformed
Of nuptial sanctity and marriage rites;
Grace was in all her steps, heaven in her eye,
In every gesture dignity and love.
I, overjoyed, could not forbear aloud:
   ' "This turn hath made amends; thou hast fulfilled
Thy words, creator bounteous and benign,
Giver of all things fair – but fairest this
Of all thy gifts – nor enviest. I now see
Bone of my bone, flesh of my flesh, my self
Before me; woman is her name, of man
Extracted; for this cause he shall forgo
Father and mother, and to his wife adhere,
And they shall be one flesh, one heart, one soul."

'She heard me thus, and, though divinely brought,
Yet innocence and virgin modesty,
Her virtue and the conscience of her worth,
That would be wooed, and not unsought be won,
Not obvious, not obtrusive, but retired,
The more desirable – or, to say all,
Nature herself, though pure of sinful thought –
Wrought in her so, that seeing me, she turned;
I followed her; she what was honour knew,
And with obsequious majesty approved
My pleaded reason. To the nuptial bower
I led her blushing like the morn; all heaven,
And happy constellations, on that hour
Shed their selectest influence; the earth
Gave sign of gratulation, and each hill;
Joyous the birds; fresh gales and gentle airs
Whispered it to the woods, and from their wings
Flung rose, flung odours from the spicy shrub,
Disporting, till the amorous bird of night
Sung spousal, and bid haste the evening star
On his hill-top to light the bridal lamp.

(Lines 460–520)

To whom the angel, with contracted brow:
'Accuse not nature, she hath done her part;
Do thou but thine, and be not diffident
Of wisdom; she deserts thee not, if thou
Dismiss not her, when most thou need'st her nigh,
By attributing overmuch to things
Less excellent, as thou thyself perceiv'st.
For, what admir'st thou, what transports thee so,
An outside? Fair, no doubt, and worthy well
Thy cherishing, thy honouring, and thy love,
Not thy subjection; weigh with her thyself;
Then value; oft-times nothing profits more
Than self-esteem, grounded on just and right
Well managed; of that skill the more thou know'st,
The more she will acknowledge thee her head,
And to realities yield all her shows –
Made so adorn for thy delight the more,
So awful, that with honour thou may'st love
Thy mate, who sees when thou art seen least wise.
But if the sense of touch whereby mankind
Is propagated seem such dear delight
Beyond all other, think the same vouchsafed
To cattle and each beast; which would not be
To them made common and divulged, if aught
Therein enjoyed were worthy to subdue
The soul of man, or passion in him move.
What higher in her society thou find'st

Attractive, human, rational, love still:
In loving thou dost well; in passion not,
Wherein true love consists not; love refines
The thoughts, and heart enlarges – hath his seat
In reason, and is judicious, is the scale
By which to heavenly love thou may'st ascend,
Not sunk in carnal pleasure; for which cause
Among the beasts no mate for thee was found.'

(Lines 560–594)

BOOK IX

THE ARGUMENT

Satan, having compassed the earth, with meditated guile returns as a mist by night into Paradise; enters into the serpent sleeping. Adam and Eve in the morning go forth to their labours, which Eve proposes to divide in several places, each labouring apart: Adam consents not, alleging the danger lest that enemy of whom they were forewarned should attempt her found alone; Eve, loath to be thought not circumspect or firm enough, urges her going apart, the rather desirous to make trial of her strength; Adam at last yields; the serpent finds her alone: his subtle approach, first gazing, then speaking, with much flattery extolling Eve above all other creatures. Eve, wondering to hear the serpent speak, asks how he attained to human speech and such understanding not till now; the serpent answers that by tasting of a certain tree in the garden he attained both to speech and reason, till then void of both; Eve requires him to bring her to that tree, and finds it to be the tree of knowledge forbidden: the serpent, now grown bolder, with many wiles and arguments induces her at length to eat; she, pleased with the taste, deliberates a while whether to impart thereof to Adam or not; at last brings him of the fruit; relates what persuaded her to eat thereof; Adam, at

first amazed, but perceiving her lost, resolves, through
vehemence of love, to perish with her, and extenuating
the trespass, eats also of the fruit; the effects thereof
in them both; they seek to cover their nakedness; then
fall to variance and accusation of one another.

*

'What may this mean? Language of man
    pronounced
By tongue of brute, and human sense expressed?
The first at least of these I thought denied
To beasts, whom God on their creation-day
Created mute to all articulate sound;
The latter I demur, for in their looks
Much reason, and in their actions, oft appears.
Thee, serpent, subtlest beast of all the field
I knew, but not with human voice endued;
Redouble then this miracle, and say,
How cam'st thou speakable of mute, and how
To me so friendly grown above the rest
Of brutal kind that daily are in sight:
Say, for such wonder claims attention due.'
  To whom the guileful tempter thus replied:
'Empress of this fair world, resplendent Eve,
Easy to me it is to tell thee all
What thou command'st, and right thou shouldst
    be obeyed;

I was at first as other beasts that graze
The trodden herb, of abject thoughts and low,
As was my food, nor aught but food discerned
Or sex, and apprehended nothing high:
Till on a day, roving the field, I chanced
A goodly tree far distant to behold,
Loaden with fruit of fairest colours mixed,
Ruddy and gold; I nearer drew to gaze,
When from the boughs a savoury odour blown,
Grateful to appetite, more pleased my sense
Than smell of sweetest fennel, or the teats
Of ewe or goat dropping with milk at even,
Unsucked of lamb or kid, that tend their play.
To satisfy the sharp desire I had
Of tasting those fair apples, I resolved
Not to defer; hunger and thirst at once,
Powerful persuaders, quickened at the scent
Of that alluring fruit, urged me so keen.
About the mossy trunk I wound me soon,
For, high from ground, the branches would require
Thy utmost reach, or Adam's: round the tree
All other beasts that saw, with like desire
Longing and envying stood, but could not reach.
Amid the tree now got, where plenty hung
Tempting so nigh, to pluck and eat my fill
I spared not, for such pleasure till that hour
At feed or fountain never had I found.

Sated at length, ere long I might perceive
Strange alteration in me, to degree
Of reason in my inward powers, and speech
Wanted not long, though to this shape retained.
Thenceforth to speculations high or deep
I turned my thoughts, and with capacious mind
Considered all things visible in heaven,
Or earth, or middle, all things fair and good;
But all that fair and good in thy divine
Semblance and in thy beauty's heavenly ray,
United I beheld – no fair to thine
Equivalent or second; which compelled
Me thus, though importune perhaps, to come
And gaze, and worship thee of right declared
Sovereign of creatures, universal dame.'

(Lines 553–612)

*

So saying, her rash hand in evil hour
Forth reaching to the fruit, she plucked, she ate;
Earth felt the wound, and nature from her seat,
Sighing through all her works, gave signs of woe
That all was lost. Back to the thicket slunk
The guilty serpent, and well might, for Eve,
Intent now only on her taste, naught else
Regarded; such delight till then, as seemed,

In fruit she never tasted, whether true,
Or fancied so through expectation high
Of knowledge; nor was godhead from her thought.
Greedily she engorged without restraint,
And knew not eating death; satiate at length,
And heightened as with wine, jocund and boon,
Thus to herself she pleasingly began:
    'O sovereign, virtuous, precious of all trees
In Paradise, of operation blest
To sapience, hitherto obscured, infamed,
And thy fair fruit let hang, as to no end
Created; but henceforth my early care,
Not without song, each morning, and due praise,
Shall tend thee, and the fertile burden ease
Of thy full branches, offered free to all;
Till dieted by thee I grow mature
In knowledge, as the gods who all things know;
Though others envy what they cannot give –
For had the gift been theirs, it had not here
Thus grown. Experience, next to thee I owe,
Best guide: not following thee, I had remained
In ignorance; thou open'st wisdom's way,
And giv'st access, though secret she retire.
And I perhaps am secret: heaven is high –
High, and remote to see from thence distinct
Each thing on earth; and other care perhaps
May have diverted from continual watch

Our great forbidder, safe with all his spies
About him. But to Adam in what sort
Shall I appear? Shall I to him make known
As yet my change, and give him to partake
Full happiness with me, or rather not,
But keep the odds of knowledge in my power
Without copartner? So to add what wants
In female sex, the more to draw his love,
And render me more equal, and perhaps –
A thing not undesirable – sometime
Superior; for, inferior, who is free?
This may be well; but what if God have seen,
And death ensue? Then I shall be no more;
And Adam, wedded to another Eve,
Shall live with her enjoying, I extinct;
A death to think. Confirmed, then, I resolve
Adam shall share with me in bliss or woe;
So dear I love him that with him all deaths
I could endure, without him live no life.'

(Lines 780–833)

BOOK X

Man's transgression known, the guardian angels for-
sake Paradise, and return up to heaven to approve
their vigilance, and are approved; God declaring that
the entrance of Satan could not be by them prevented.
He sends his Son to judge the transgressors; who
descends, and gives sentence accordingly; then, in pity,
clothes them both, and reascends. Sin and Death
sitting till then at the gates of hell, by wondrous
sympathy feeling the success of Satan in this new
world, and the sin by man there committed, resolve
to sit no longer confined in hell, but to follow Satan,
their sire, up to the place of man: to make the way
easier from hell to this world to and fro, they pave a
broad highway or bridge over chaos, according to the
track that Satan first made; then, preparing for earth,
they meet him, proud of his success, returning to hell;
their mutual gratulation. Satan arrives at Pandemon-
ium; in full assembly relates, with boasting, his success
against man; instead of applause is entertained with a
general hiss by all his audience, transformed, with
himself also, suddenly into serpents, according to his
doom given in Paradise; then, deluded with a show of
the forbidden tree springing up before them, they,
greedily reaching to take of the fruit, chew dust and

bitter ashes. The proceedings of Sin and Death: God foretells the final victory of his Son over them, and the renewing of all things; but, for the present, commands his angels to make several alterations in the heavens and elements. Adam, more and more perceiving his fallen condition, heavily bewails, rejects the condolement of Eve; she persists, and at length appeases him: then, to evade the curse likely to fall on their offspring, proposes to Adam violent ways which he approves not, but, conceiving better hope, puts her in mind of the late promise made them, that her seed should be revenged on the serpent, and exhorts her, with him, to seek peace of the offended Deity by repentance and supplication.

*

'Thrones, dominations, princedoms, virtues, powers,
For in possession such, not only of right,
I call ye, and declare ye now, returned
Successful beyond hope, to lead ye forth
Triumphant out of this infernal pit
Abominable, accursed, the house of woe,
And dungeon of our tyrant; now possess,
As lords, a spacious world, to our native heaven
Little inferior, by my adventure hard
With peril great achieved. Long were to tell
What I have done, what suffered, with what pain

Voyaged the unreal, vast, unbounded deep
Of horrible confusion – over which
By Sin and Death a broad way now is paved,
To expedite your glorious march; but I
Toiled out my uncouth passage, forced to ride
The untractable abyss, plunged in the womb
Of unoriginal Night and Chaos wild,
That, jealous of their secrets, fiercely opposed
My journey strange, with clamorous uproar
Protesting fate supreme; thence how I found
The new-created world, which fame in heaven
Long had foretold, a fabric wonderful,
Of absolute perfection; therein man
Placed in a paradise, by our exile
Made happy; him by fraud I have seduced
From his creator, and the more to increase
Your wonder, with an apple; he, thereat
Offended – worth your laughter – hath given up
Both his beloved man and all his world
To Sin and Death a prey, and so to us,
Without our hazard, labour, or alarm,
To range in, and to dwell, and over man
To rule, as over all he should have ruled.
True is, me also he hath judged; or rather
Me not, but the brute serpent in whose shape
Man I deceived; that which to me belongs
Is enmity, which he will put between

Me and mankind: I am to bruise his heel;
His seed – when, is not set – shall bruise my head;
A world who would not purchase with a bruise,
Or much more grievous pain? Ye have the account
Of my performance; what remains, ye gods,
But up and enter now into full bliss?'
    So having said, a while he stood, expecting
Their universal shout and high applause
To fill his ear; when, contrary, he hears,
On all sides, from innumerable tongues
A dismal universal hiss, the sound
Of public scorn; he wondered, but not long
Had leisure, wondering at himself now more;
His visage drawn he felt to sharp and spare,
His arms clung to his ribs, his legs entwining
Each other, till supplanted down he fell,
A monstrous serpent on his belly prone,
Reluctant, but in vain; a greater power
Now ruled him, punished in the shape he sinned,
According to his doom; he would have spoke,
But hiss for hiss returned with forked tongue
To forked tongue; for now were all transformed
Alike, to serpents all, as accessories
To his bold riot; dreadful was the din
Of hissing through the hall, thick-swarming now
With complicated monsters, head and tail –
Scorpion, and asp, and amphisbaena dire,

Cerastes horned, hydrus, and ellops drear,
And dipsas (not so thick swarmed once the soil
Bedropped with blood of Gorgon, or the isle
Ophiusa); but still greatest he the midst,
Now dragon grown, larger than whom the sun
Engendered in the Pythian vale on slime,
Huge python; and his power no less he seemed
Above the rest still to retain; they all
Him followed, issuing forth to the open field,
Where all yet left of that revolted rout,
Heaven-fallen, in station stood or just array,
Sublime with expectation when to see
In triumph issuing forth their glorious chief;
They saw, but other sight instead – a crowd
Of ugly serpents; horror on them fell,
And horrid sympathy; for what they saw
They felt themselves now changing; down their arms,
Down fell both spear and shield; down they as fast,
And the dire hiss renewed, and the dire form
Catched by contagion, like in punishment
As in their crime. Thus was the applause they meant
Turned to exploding hiss, triumph to shame
Cast on themselves from their own mouths. There
        stood
A grove hard by, sprung up with this their change,
His will who reigns above, to aggravate
Their penance, laden with fair fruit, like that

Which grew in Paradise, the bait of Eve
Used by the tempter; on that prospect strange
Their earnest eyes they fixed, imagining
For one forbidden tree a multitude
Now risen, to work them further woe or shame;
Yet parched with scalding thirst and hunger fierce,
Though to delude them sent, could not abstain,
But on they rolled in heaps, and up the trees
Climbing, sat thicker than the snaky locks
That curled Megaera; greedily they plucked
The fruitage fair to sight, like that which grew
Near that bituminous lake where Sodom flamed;
This, more delusive, not the touch, but taste
Deceived; they, fondly thinking to allay
Their appetite with gust, instead of fruit
Chewed bitter ashes, which the offended taste
With spattering noise rejected; oft they assayed,
Hunger and thirst constraining; drugged as oft,
With hatefulest disrelish writhed their jaws
With soot and cinders filled; so oft they fell
Into the same illusion, not as man
Whom they triumphed once lapsed. Thus were
            they plagued,
And worn with famine long, and ceaseless hiss,
Till their lost shape, permitted, they resumed –
Yearly enjoined, some say, to undergo
This annual humbling certain numbered days,

To dash their pride, and joy for man seduced.
However, some tradition they dispersed
Among the heathen of their purchase got,
And fabled how the serpent, whom they called
Ophion, with Eurynome – the wide-
Encroaching Eve perhaps – had first the rule
Of high Olympus, thence by Saturn driven
And Ops, ere yet Dictaean Jove was born.

(Lines 460–584)

BOOK XI

THE ARGUMENT

The Son of God presents to his Father the prayers of
our first parents now repenting, and intercedes for
them; God accepts them, but declares that they must
no longer abide in Paradise; sends Michael with a
band of cherubim to dispossess them but first to reveal
to Adam future things: Michael's coming down. Adam
shows to Eve certain ominous signs: he discerns
Michael's approach; goes out to meet him: the angel
denounces their departure. Eve's lamentation. Adam
pleads, but submits; the angel leads him up to a high
hill; sets before him in vision what shall happen till
the flood.

*

'Adam, now ope thine eyes, and first behold
The effects which thy original crime hath wrought
In some to spring from thee, who never touched
The excepted tree, nor with the snake conspired,
Nor sinned thy sin, yet from that sin derive
Corruption to bring forth more violent deeds.'
　His eyes he opened, and beheld a field,
Part arable and tilth, whereon were sheaves
New-reaped, the other part sheep-walks and folds;
I' the midst an altar as the landmark stood,

Rustic, of grassy sward; thither anon
A sweaty reaper from his tillage brought
First-fruits, the green ear and the yellow sheaf,
Unculled, as came to hand; a shepherd next,
More meek, came with the firstlings of his flock,
Choicest and best; then sacrificing, laid
The inwards and their fat, with incense strewed,
On the cleft wood, and all due rites performed.
His offering soon propitious fire from heaven
Consumed, with nimble glance and grateful steam;
The other's not, for his was not sincere:
Whereat he inly raged, and as they talked,
Smote him into the midriff with a stone
That beat out life; he fell, and deadly pale,
Groaned out his soul, with gushing blood effused.
Much at that sight was Adam in his heart
Dismayed, and thus in haste to the angel cried:
    'O teacher, some great mischief hath befallen
To that meek man, who well had sacrificed;
Is piety thus and pure devotion paid?'
    To whom Michael thus, he also moved, replied:
'These two are brethren, Adam, and to come
Out of thy loins; the unjust the just hath slain,
For envy that his brother's offering found
From heaven acceptance; but the bloody fact
Will be avenged, and the other's faith approved
Lose no reward, though here thou see him die,

Rolling in dust and gore.' To which our sire:
    'Alas, both for the deed and for the cause!
But have I now seen death? Is this the way
I must return to native dust? O sight
Of terror, foul and ugly to behold;
Horrid to think, how horrible to feel!'
    To whom thus Michael: 'Death thou hast seen
In his first shape on man; but many shapes
Of Death, and many are the ways that lead
To his grim cave – all dismal, yet to sense
More terrible at the entrance than within.
Some, as thou saw'st, by violent stroke shall die,
By fire, flood, famine; by intemperance more
In meats and drinks, which on the earth shall bring
Diseases dire, of which a monstrous crew
Before thee shall appear, that thou may'st know
What misery the inabstinence of Eve
Shall bring on men.' Immediately a place
Before his eyes appeared, sad, noisome, dark;
A lazar-house it seemed, wherein were laid
Numbers of all diseased – all maladies
Of ghastly spasm, or racking torture, qualms
Of heart-sick agony, all feverous kinds,
Convulsions, epilepsies, fierce catarrhs,
Intestine stone and ulcer, colic pangs,
Demoniac frenzy, moping melancholy,
And moon-struck madness, pining atrophy,

Marasmus, and wide-wasting pestilence,
Dropsies and asthmas, and joint-racking rheums.
Dire was the tossing, deep the groans; Despair
Tended the sick, busiest from couch to couch;
And over them triumphant Death his dart
Shook, but delayed to strike, though oft invoked
With vows, as their chief good and final hope.
Sight so deform what heart of rock could long
Dry-eyed behold? Adam could not, but wept,
Though not of woman born: compassion quelled
His best of man, and gave him up to tears
A space, till firmer thoughts restrained excess,
And, scarce recovering words, his plaint renewed:
    'O miserable mankind, to what fall
Degraded, to what wretched state reserved!
Better end here unborn. Why is life given
To be thus wrested from us? Rather why
Obtruded on us thus? Who, if we knew
What we receive, would either not accept
Life offered, or soon beg to lay it down,
Glad to be so dismissed in peace. Can thus
The image of God in man, created once
So goodly and erect, though faulty since,
To such unsightly sufferings be debased
Under inhuman pains? Why should not man,
Retaining still divine similitude
In part, from such deformities be free,

And for his maker's image sake exempt?'
   'Their maker's image,' answered Michael, 'then
Forsook them, when themselves they vilified
To serve ungoverned appetite, and took
His image whom they served – a brutish vice,
Inductive mainly to the sin of Eve.
Therefore so abject is their punishment,
Disfiguring not God's likeness, but their own;
Or if his likeness, by themselves defaced
While they pervert pure nature's healthful rules
To loathsome sickness – worthily, since they
God's image did not reverence in themselves.'

                        (Lines 423–525)

              *

   He looked, and saw a spacious plain, whereon
Were tents of various hue: by some were herds
Of cattle grazing: others whence the sound
Of instruments that made melodious chime
Was heard, of harp and organ, and who moved
Their stops and chords was seen: his volant touch
Instinct through all proportions low and high
Fled and pursued transverse the resonant fugue.
In other part stood one who, at the forge
Labouring, two massy clods of iron and brass
Had melted (whether found where casual fire

Had wasted woods, on mountain or in vale,
Down to the veins of earth, thence gliding hot
To some cave's mouth, or whether washed by stream
From underground); the liquid ore he drained
Into fit moulds prepared; from which he formed
First his own tools, then what might else be wrought
Fusile or graven in metal. After these,
But on the hither side, a different sort
From the high neighbouring hills, which was their seat,
Down to the plain descended: by their guise
Just men they seemed, and all their study bent
To worship God aright, and know his works
Not hid, nor those things last which might preserve
Freedom and peace to men; they on the plain
Long had not walked when from the tents behold
A bevy of fair women, richly gay
In gems and wanton dress; to the harp they sung
Soft amorous ditties, and in dance came on;
The men, though grave, eyed them, and let their eyes
Rove without rein, till, in the amorous net
Fast caught, they liked, and each his liking chose;
And now of love they treat, till the evening star,
Love's harbinger, appeared; then all in heat,
They light the nuptial torch, and bid invoke
Hymen, then first to marriage rites invoked:
With feast and music all the tents resound.
Such happy interview, and fair event

Of love and youth not lost, songs, garlands, flowers,
And charming symphonies, attached the heart
Of Adam, soon inclined to admit delight,
The bent of nature; which he thus expressed:

'True opener of mine eyes, prime angel blest,
Much better seems this vision, and more hope
Of peaceful days portends, than those two past:
Those were of hate and death, or pain much worse;
Here nature seems fulfilled in all her ends.'

(Lines 556–602)

*

He looked, and saw the ark hull on the flood,
Which now abated; for the clouds were fled,
Driven by a keen north-wind, that blowing dry,
Wrinkled the face of deluge, as decayed;
And the clear sun on his wide watery glass
Gazed hot, and of the fresh wave largely drew,
As after thirst; which made their flowing shrink
From standing lake to tripping ebb, that stole
With soft foot towards the deep, who now had stopped
His sluices, as the heaven his windows shut.
The ark no more now floats, but seems on ground,
Fast on the top of some high mountain fixed.
And now the tops of hills as rocks appear;
With clamour thence the rapid currents drive

Towards the retreating sea their furious tide.
Forthwith from out the ark a raven flies,
And after him, the surer messenger,
A dove sent forth once and again to spy
Green tree or ground whereon his foot may light;
The second time returning, in his bill
An olive-leaf he brings, pacific sign;
Anon dry ground appears, and from his ark
The ancient sire descends, with all his train;
Then with uplifted hands, and eyes devout,
Grateful to heaven, over his head beholds
A dewy cloud, and in the cloud a bow
Conspicuous with three listed colours gay,
Betokening peace from God, and covenant new.
Whereat the heart of Adam, erst so sad,
Greatly rejoiced, and thus his joy broke forth:
    'O thou, who future things canst represent
As present, heavenly instructor, I revive
At this last sight, assured that man shall live,
With all the creatures, and their seed preserve.
Far less I now lament for one whole world
Of wicked sons destroyed, than I rejoice
For one man found so perfect, and so just,
That God vouchsafes to raise another world
From him, and all his anger to forget.
But say, what mean those coloured streaks in heaven,
Distended as the brow of God appeased?

Or serve they as a flowery verge to bind
The fluid skirts of that same watery cloud,
Lest it again dissolve and shower the earth?'
　　To whom the archangel: 'Dextrously thou aim'st;
So willingly doth God remit his ire:
Though late repenting him of man depraved,
Grieved at his heart, when looking down he saw
The whole earth filled with violence, and all flesh
Corrupting each their way; yet those removed,
Such grace shall one just man find in his sight
That he relents, not to blot out mankind,
And makes a covenant never to destroy
The earth again by flood, nor let the sea
Surpass his bounds, nor rain to drown the world
With man therein or beast; but when he brings
Over the earth a cloud, will therein set
His triple-coloured bow, whereon to look
And call to mind his covenant; day and night,
Seed-time and harvest, heat and hoary frost,
Shall hold their course, till fire purge all things new,
Both heaven and earth, wherein the just shall dwell.'

(Lines 840–901)

BOOK XII

The angel Michael continues, from the flood, to relate
what shall succeed; then, in the mention of Abraham,
comes by degrees to explain who that seed of the
woman shall be which was promised Adam and Eve
in the fall: his incarnation, death, resurrection, and
ascension; the state of the Church till his second
coming. Adam, greatly satisfied and recomforted by
these relations and promises, descends the hill with
Michael; wakens Eve, who all this while had slept, but
with gentle dreams composed to quietness of mind
and submission. Michael in either hand leads them out
of Paradise, the fiery sword waving behind them, and
the cherubim taking their stations to guard the place.

*

'O goodness infinite, goodness immense,
That all this good of evil shall produce,
And evil turn to good – more wonderful
Than that which by creation first brought forth
Light out of darkness! Full of doubt I stand,
Whether I should repent me now of sin
By me done and occasioned, or rejoice
Much more that much more good thereof
        shall spring –

To God more glory, more good-will to men
From God – and over wrath grace shall abound.
But say, if our deliverer up to heaven
Must reascend, what will betide the few,
His faithful, left among the unfaithful herd,
The enemies of truth? Who then shall guide
His people, who defend? Will they not deal
Worse with his followers than with him they dealt?'
　　'Be sure they will,' said the angel; 'but from heaven
He to his own a Comforter will send,
The promise of the Father, who shall dwell,
His Spirit within them, and the law of faith
Working through love upon their hearts shall write,
To guide them in all truth, and also arm
With spiritual armour, able to resist
Satan's assaults, and quench his fiery darts –
What man can do against them not afraid,
Though to the death; against such cruelties
With inward consolations recompensed,
And oft supported so as shall amaze
Their proudest persecutors; for the Spirit,
Poured first on his apostles, whom he sends
To evangelize the nations, then on all
Baptized, shall them with wondrous gifts endue
To speak all tongues, and do all miracles,
As did their Lord before them. Thus they win
Great numbers of each nation to receive

With joy the tidings brought from heaven: at length,
Their ministry performed, and race well run,
Their doctrine and their story written left,
They die: but in their room, as they forewarn,
Wolves shall succeed for teachers, grievous wolves,
Who all the sacred mysteries of heaven
To their own vile advantages shall turn
Of lucre and ambition, and the truth
With superstitions and traditions taint,
Left only in those written records pure,
Though not but by the Spirit understood.
Then shall they seek to avail themselves of names,
Places, and titles, and with these to join
Secular power, though feigning still to act
By spiritual; to themselves appropriating
The Spirit of God, promised alike and given
To all believers; and from that pretence,
Spiritual laws by carnal power shall force
On every conscience – laws which none shall find
Left them enrolled, or what the Spirit within
Shall on the heart engrave. What will they then
But force the spirit of grace itself, and bind
His consort, liberty? What but unbuild
His living temples, built by faith to stand –
Their own faith, not another's? For on earth
Who against faith and conscience can be heard
Infallible? Yet many will presume:

Whence heavy persecution shall arise
On all who in the worship persevere
Of spirit and truth; the rest, far greater part,
Will deem in outward rites and specious forms
Religion satisfied; truth shall retire
Bestuck with slanderous darts, and works of faith
Rarely be found; so shall the world go on,
To good malignant, to bad men benign,
Under her own weight groaning, till the day
Appear of respiration to the just
And vengeance to the wicked, at return
Of him so lately promised to thy aid,
The woman's seed – obscurely then foretold,
Now amplier known thy Saviour and thy Lord;
Last in the clouds from heaven to be revealed
In glory of the Father, to dissolve
Satan with his perverted world; then raise
From the conflagrant mass, purged and refined,
New heavens, new earth, ages of endless date
Founded in righteousness and peace and love,
To bring forth fruits, joy and eternal bliss.'

   He ended; and thus Adam last replied:
'How soon hath thy prediction, seer blest,
Measured this transient world, the race of time,
Till time stand fixed; beyond is all abyss –
Eternity, whose end no eye can reach.
Greatly instructed I shall hence depart,

Greatly in peace of thought, and have my fill
Of knowledge, what this vessel can contain;
Beyond which was my folly to aspire.
Henceforth I learn that to obey is best,
And love with fear the only God, to walk
As in his presence, ever to observe
His providence, and on him sole depend,
Merciful over all his works, with good
Still overcoming evil, and by small
Accomplishing great things – by things deemed weak
Subverting worldly-strong, and worldly-wise
By simply meek; that suffering for truth's sake
Is fortitude to highest victory,
And to the faithful death the gate of life –
Taught this by his example whom I now
Acknowledge my Redeemer ever blest.'
  To whom thus also the angel last replied:
'This having learned, thou hast attained the sum
Of wisdom; hope no higher, though all the stars
Thou knew'st by name, and all the ethereal powers,
All secrets of the deep, all nature's works,
Or works of God in heaven, air, earth, or sea;
And all the riches of this world enjoy'dst,
And all the rule, one empire; only add
Deeds to thy knowledge answerable, add faith,
Add virtue, patience, temperance, add love,
By name to come called Charity, the soul

Of all the rest: then wilt thou not be loath
To leave this Paradise, but shalt possess
A paradise within thee, happier far.
Let us descend now, therefore, from this top
Of speculation; for the hour precise
Exacts our parting hence; and see, the guards,
By me encamped on yonder hill, expect
Their motion, at whose front a flaming sword,
In signal of remove, waves fiercely round;
We may no longer stay; go, waken Eve;
Her also I with gentle dreams have calmed,
Portending good, and all her spirits composed
To meek submission: thou at season fit
Let her with thee partake what thou hast heard –
Chiefly what may concern her faith to know,
The great deliverance by her seed to come
(For by the woman's seed) on all mankind –
That ye may live, which will be many days,
Both in one faith unanimous; though sad
With cause for evils past, yet much more cheered
With meditation on the happy end.'

   He ended, and they both descend the hill;
Descended, Adam to the bower where Eve
Lay sleeping ran before, but found her waked;
And thus with words not sad she him received:

    'Whence thou return'st and whither went'st I know;
For God is also in sleep, and dreams advise,

Which he hath sent propitious, some great good
Presaging, since, with sorrow and heart's distress
Wearied, I fell asleep; but now lead on;
In me is no delay; with thee to go
Is to stay here; without thee here to stay
Is to go hence unwilling; thou to me
Art all things under heaven, all places thou,
Who for my wilful crime art banished hence.
This further consolation yet secure
I carry hence: though all by me is lost,
Such favour I unworthy am vouchsafed,
By me the promised seed shall all restore.'
  So spake our mother Eve, and Adam heard
Well pleased, but answered not; for now too nigh
The archangel stood, and from the other hill
To their fixed station, all in bright array,
The cherubim descended, on the ground
Gliding meteorous, as evening mist
Risen from a river o'er the marish glides,
And gathers ground fast at the labourer's heel
Homeward returning. High in front advanced,
The brandished sword of God before them blazed,
Fierce as a comet; which with torrid heat,
And vapour as the Libyan air adust,
Began to parch that temperate clime; whereat
In either hand the hastening angel caught
Our lingering parents, and to the eastern gate

Led them direct, and down the cliff as fast
To the subjected plain – then disappeared.
They looking back, all the eastern side beheld
Of Paradise, so late their happy seat,
Waved over by that flaming brand; the gate
With dreadful faces thronged and fiery arms;
Some natural tears they dropped, but wiped them soon,
The world was all before them, where to choose
Their place of rest, and providence their guide;
They hand in hand with wandering steps and slow,
Through Eden took their solitary way.

(Lines 469–649)